Jeffrey K. Edwards, EdD
Anthony W. Heath, PhD

A Consumer's Guide to Mental Health Services

Unveiling the Mysteries and Secrets of Psychotherapy

Pre-publication REVIEW . . .

"Dr. Edwards and Dr. Heath have provided a rare and valuable book which comes at a crucial time in the saga of health care in America. They have written an honest, informative, and above all, useful manual for everyday people to use as a field manual to negotiate the morass of what mental health care has become in America. Particularly helpful are the vignettes that illustrate the issues in practical terms. The authors also set apart important points of information that demystify very complex clinical and political issues in 'Something You Should Know' boxes. These pity statements entice the reader to read further about these issues in their text and serve as a form of written advocate for the consumer to use when making crucial decisions. It is extremely valuable that they address issues of family and child intervention, categories that are often given little attention in the current biological, cost-driven mental/ health care industry. The authors are to be congratulated for their tenacious, entertaining, and accessible work."

John J. Schaut, PsyD
Clinical Psychologist, Stress Disorders Treatment Unit (SDTU)

A Consumer's Guide to Mental Health Services

Unveiling the Mysteries and Secrets of Psychotherapy

Terry S. Trepper, PhD
Editor

College Students in Distress: A Resource Guide for Faculty, Staff, and Campus Community by Bruce S. Sharkin

Cultural Diversity and Suicide: Ethnic, Religious, Gender, and Sexual Orientation Perspectives by Mark M. Leach

Crisis Counseling and Therapy by Jackson Rainer and Frieda Brown

A Consumer's Guide to Mental Health Services: Unveiling the Mysteries and Secrets of Psychotherapy by Jeffrey K. Edwards and Anthony W. Health

Sex-Offender Therapy: A "How-To" Workbook for Therapists Treating Sexually Aggressive Adults, Adolescents, and Children by Rudy Flora, Joseph T. Duehl, Wanda Fisher, Sandra Halsey, Michael Keohane, Barbara L. Maberry, Jeffrey A. McCorkindale, and Leroy C. Parson

A Consumer's Guide to Mental Health Services

Unveiling the Mysteries and Secrets of Psychotherapy

Jeffrey K. Edwards, EdD
Anthony W. Heath, PhD

Routledge
Taylor & Francis Group
New York London

Routledge is an imprint of the
Taylor & Francis Group, an informa business

Routledge
Taylor & Francis Group
270 Madison Avenue
New York, NY 10016

Routledge
Taylor & Francis Group
2 Park Square
Milton Park, Abingdon
Oxon OX14 4RN

Printed in the United States of America on acid-free paper
International Standard Book Number-13: 978-0-7890-3267-6 (Softcover)
Library of Congress catalog number: 2007019263
PUBLISHER'S NOTE
Identities and circumstances of individuals discussed in this book have been changed to protect confidentiality.

Cover Design by Jennifer M. Gaska

Library of Congress Cataloging-in-Publication Data

Catalog record is available from the Library of Congress

Visit the Taylor & Francis Web site at
http://www.taylorandfrancis.com

and the Routledge Web site at
http://www.routledge.com

CONTENTS

ABOUT THE AUTHORS

Jeffrey K. Edwards, EdD, LMFT, is Professor of Counselor Education at Northeastern Illinois University. His work focuses on family therapy, clinical supervision, sex therapy, and substance abuse therapy. A therapist and clinical supervisor both in private practice and at mental health agencies, residential treatment centers, and day treatment centers for over 39 years, Dr. Edwards has published extensively in many areas of counseling and has given national workshops on clinical supervision.

Anthony W. Heath, PhD, is Regional Director, Quality Improvement for United Behavioral Health in Schaumburg, Illinois, which supports more than 43 million insured people nationwide. A former director of Northern Illinois University's graduate program in family therapy, Dr. Heath has given over 300 presentations to professionals and the public, written two books, and authored more than 65 journal articles and book chapters.

Foreword

You hold in your hands one of the first guides for mental health services for consumers ever printed. It is unbiased. That means it hasn't been written by a special-interest group. Or some group's lobbying efforts. So, it provides multiple views of just what can be helpful when you're looking for help. Consumers saddled with a problem, either their own or that of a loved one, need unbiased information, or should certainly want it. They need to have the ability to make decisions that will help, not frustrate. The media bombard us constantly about information on new treatments, information that can be both biased *and* misleading. What you hear is often contradictory and confusing:

Is medication necessary? What about side effects? Can it make you do things you don't want to do? Who do you see for a problem? What's a counselor? Is that different from a social worker? Or a psychiatrist? That's the kind of stuff you'll find in this book—and more.

About now, you're probably asking yourself: why is a sportscaster writing a Foreword for a book on mental health? Skip the obvious joke. I know this book is needed. I am, in no way, associated with the mental health industry or any of its giant corporate psychopharmacology groups, nor am I with any of the numerous clinicians who are competing for your dollar. I am, in a word, unbiased. I've seen folks of all sorts who could use both brief and long-term help. I've seen how family problems—divorce, substance abuse, mental anguish—can affect lives, and livelihoods. As a spokesman and longtime volunteer for the March of Dimes, I know firsthand how good and timely information can help individuals and families in need of services. Why search blindly through phone books or rely on the next TV commercial? This is a book that might have all the answers you need.

Mental health treatment can be costly, no question about it. Many Americans don't get quality service, and with the rising costs of health care, there will be many more left without care. This book suggests alternatives. It's a tell-all about where and how to get good care at reasonable rates. When mediation is expensive, and extended private counseling is even more so, this book is a pretty good idea, don't you think?

Greg Gumbel

Introduction

> If there is one message writ large within the annals of anthropology, it is to beware the solid truths of one's own culture. If we contrast our views with those of others, we find that what we take to be "reliable knowledge" is more properly considered a form of folklore.
>
> Kenneth J. Gergen (1991)

If you've ever tried to find help for emotional distress, a major life transition, depression, anxiety, and have been overwhelmed and confused by your choices, you are not alone. There are over 260 counseling/psychotherapy models used to treat emotional problems or serious mental illnesses, and most of us have only vague recommendations from friends to go on.[1,2] The insurance companies and their complicated limitations on care only make matters more confusing. Even the language we use to describe states of mental health can be problematic. "Mental health," "mental illness," "behavioral health care," "emotionally disturbed"—this is language that is difficult to understand, frightening, and may seem derogatory. In the midst of all this, how do you know where to look for the right services? Who should you see: a psychiatrist, social worker, counselor, or a psychologist? And how do you find the right one?

We wrote this book to help you navigate the quagmire of services. The first three chapters describe how the three main models and the clinicians who use them view mental health in the first place. In Chapter 4 we'll look at the various players—social workers, psychologists, psychiatrists, counselors, etc.—and then in Chapters 5 and 6 we will look at the types of services they provide, both talk therapies as well as medications. In Chapter 7 we'll look at the ethical codes of all professions and what your rights are as consumers. Chapter 8 looks at how the insurance industry began and how it became such an important component of managed mental health care. Finally, because we passionately believe that most people do *not* need years of therapy to resolve their problems, we devote the last chapter to helping you discover what's right for you with our "Spectrum of Services and Products for Mental Health Concerns." We will discuss possible alternatives to years of therapy—forming self-help groups, speaking with a clergyperson, or developing a supportive intentional community—and how you can find the right "clinical consultant" for your particular concerns. We have even included a list of questions you can use as you interview prospective clinicians, to help empower you to get care that's right for you.

Our great hope is that you use this book! If you are in immediate crisis, use it as a reference or resource book. There is information about practices, professionals, ethics, alternatives, and helpful suggestions that will make your search less confusing. If you are only beginning to contemplate finding services for yourself or someone you love, then read the book cover to cover, and be a well-informed mental health consumer. Most of all, use the key questions in the last chapter to interview a potential clinician so you can find a good fit.

Before we launch into a description of the players, ethics, treatment options, and the like, we'd like to note some of the most serious problems besetting the system of mental health; we don't think you can make an informed decision for your own care without understanding the social, economic, and political aspects involved.

First of all, the language of mental health is a holdover from the days when most human problems were considered to be medical conditions. There is still much debate over this, but the biological-medical model still dominates. As you will see, this is no accident but rather a situation with political and economic causes. Shifts in the way we understand human behavior—paradigm shifts—are common in this field. Yet there have been, and continue to be, alternative points of view about what causes human dilemmas and their treatment. In addition, because mental health is associated with strong emotional words—mental illness, psychopathology, instability—you may be restrained from making good decisions for yourself or a loved one. A common myth, another holdover from psychoanalytic days, is that the client should remain in treatment until she or he is completely cured. Today, a better metaphor is that one should expect life to always have problems, and that some need professional help. So, psychotherapy or counseling is better approached as if one were going to see a dentist. Sometimes you go for a serious problem, other times for a cleaning or checkup.

Remember, too, that mental health care is a smaller piece of the larger health care system in the United States. Like its "bigger sister," it has flaws, is primarily for the middle and upper class, and provides coverage if you have qualifying insurance (and even then there is most likely a hefty co-pay and limits); and like health care, the poor suffer disproportionately, even though they, as the most disenfranchised, are often the most in need.

Taking what is given to you without knowing all the choices, subtleties, and possibilities forces you into a default position. Being a good mental health consumer requires a bit of active inquiry on your part, so know your choices and understand your options!

PART I: CAUSES OF MENTAL HEALTH PROBLEMS

My father (Jeff) used to tell an old joke that goes, "mental illness is contagious, you catch it from your kids." Ever since I heard him say that I wondered how people's problems come about. Well, over the years and years that people have attempted to find the answers to this, many paradigms—beliefs about the answer to this question— have come about, changed, and been argued about by those who study and practice in the field of mental health. The three prominent models, biological (Chapter 1), psychological (Chapter 2), and family systems (Chapter 3), are presented here in Part I, as well as the pros and cons of the models' uses.

Even models that claim to be integrative still maintain a preference for a hierarchy of cause, most often these days defaulting to the biological model as the most popular method of quick and easy treatment. Although this is better than what early practitioners believed to be the cause, sin, and immoral living, we have noted the many problems that occur when guilds of clinicians who have financial stakes in their beliefs try to marginalize one another.

People are complex; they have their own beliefs about what can and cannot help. It is time to look at these models in full, and find alternatives that will assure you will receive care that:

- Helps resolve your problem in a timely fashion
- Considers your situation holistically, biologically, psychologically, and systemically
- Provides affirming messages regarding your ability to transcend your problems
- Treats you with dignity and respect, as an equal partner in your treatment

It is with this intent that this book has been written: to open for scrutiny the models and conflicting views as well as possibilities for change that may hide behind the veil.

Chapter 1

The Medical Model

> The disease model concentrates on a narrow range of "diseases," those that fall comfortably into the physician and medication realm, and it ignores other, even more harmful states.
>
> Martin E.P. Seligman (2001)

When push comes to shove, currently there are only two types of treatment being used in mental health—medication and talk therapy, each with many models of use. Therefore, it is important that you understand them so that you can make the right choice(s) for your own care. Just as trying to address a physical problem can have you seeing several different kinds of professionals, all of whom have differing views, so it is with mental health. There are many models, all of which can be helpful some of the time. It is up to you to investigate your options and make the choice that is best for your situation.

First, let us make a few clarifying points about terms. The words *therapy, psychotherapy,* and *counseling* are used interchangeably in the field, even though there are many professionals who prefer one word over the other. Several studies have examined the supposed differences between them; most conclude that psychotherapy and those who practice it are no more helpful than those who do counseling. In other words, even though the myth that one is better than the other persists, it appears that the rose is the same by any name. It is important that you understand that whoever you choose to see is biased about what they do and why it is best.

Next, though we are talking about practitioners in several distinct professions—psychologists, social workers, counselors, psychiatrists, etc., to simplify things, we have elected to call them all *clinicians.* We will talk more about each of the different professions in Chapter 2, to help you understand the field better. Also, we have chosen to call people who go to see a clinician *clients,* even though many clinicians prefer the term *patients.* We find the word *patient* to be too loaded, too medically oriented.

That's also why we prefer the term *mental health concerns* to *mental illness, emotional disturbance,* or some such. People go to see clinicians for many types of problems, most of which are not medical at all.

THE BIOLOGICAL MEDICAL MODEL

Let's start with the model presently in vogue—the biological model. If you have ever had a headache or backache and immediately reached for over-the-counter medication, you understand that we are a quick-fix culture. We know that stress and environmental factors can cause headaches and backaches and that aspirin can be dangerous if taken to excess or for the wrong reasons, but still, we want to end the pain. The same holds true in the treatment of other human dilemmas (see Box 1.1). The current culture of mental health and counseling services most often emphasizes the biological, as is evident from the insurance industry's requirement that clinicians use the *Diagnostic and Statistical Manual of Mental Disorders* (DSM IV-TR) of the American Psychiatric Association (APA) in diagnosing clients. No DSM IV-TR diagnosis, no payment for services. This model rests on the idea that specific medications or treatments can be established for each specific type of problem. As if one size really could fit all. This model has many critics and flaws, as it relies on statistics and probability, which simply don't always jive with the profound variation in human experience.

BOX 1.1
The Politics of Mental Health

A common misconception is that a classification of mental disorders classifies people, when actually what are being classified are disorders that people have. (*Source:* APA, 2000, p. xxxi)

CULTURAL BIAS

Many cultures have different beliefs about health and disease. Our Western version of health and illness has tended to view these other cultural ideas as wrong. This prejudicial view has left out many possibilities for understanding and getting help. Culture will many times influence whether a symptom is even considered a problem. Psychoanalyst Karen Horney pointed out years ago that to label people as psychotic because they claimed to have visions in the midst of sacred rituals would be incorrect.[1] Culture and language can change the context and understanding of many events or behaviors modern clinicians might see as pathological.

TO MEDICATE OR NOT TO MEDICATE

Medications for psychological problems have been around for decades, and have been a boon to many people. That doesn't mean they are always the best treatment.

The many medical professionals and pharmaceutical companies work hard to promote and provide quick fixes—to the point that many of us no longer recognize that there are other options.

We have been lulled into believing that if a pill can "take care of things," that's the best way to go. It is important to have information and perspective on this rather than accept medications you may not need. Many medications are expensive and can have severe side effects, so their use must be weighed carefully against the costs.

BOX 1.2
Something You Should Know

Connections in the brain shape the way we think, but the flip side is also true. The way you think can change your brain. When you think about it, you can understand almost every mental health problem—anxiety, depression, eating disorders, personality disorder, thinking disorders—as an issue of self-regulation. Self-regulation is the balanced and integrated flow of energy and information through the major systems of the brain—brain stem, limbic circuits, neocortex, autonomic nervous system—and between one brain and another. (*Source:* Seigel cited in Wylie, 2004)

BRAIN AND MIND

The medical model rests on the idea that medications pinpoint the area in the brain that is causing the problem. This is a mechanistic view, looking at the brain—its chemistry and functions—rather than a "mind" that contains thoughts and feelings as the area in need of "fixing." We are not suggesting that we should not look at the brain, but exciting new research involves a shift in perspective away from seeing the brain as merely a chemical and neurological organ, toward its capability for rewiring itself based on its human interactions. The mind takes the brain's experience and *makes sense of it*. Far more than a simple lump of matter that responds with chemicals and synaptic firings, the brain/mind is a living, changing organism that uses its components to understand, make sense of, and relate. [2]

As psychiatry marches along in its belief that the brain of a person with emotional problems is governed only by neurons and chemicals that are in some way pathological, Siegel's work produces hope and renewed interest in seeing the brain holistically.

A BRIEF HISTORY

The assumption that biology is the only cause of human dilemmas has deep roots. Traced back to the nineteenth century, with neurology and psychiatry (see Chapter 4) treating hysteria, it was Freud's "talking cure" in the late 1800s that launched the practice of counseling as a "medical" method for treating mental health problems.

The American Psychiatric Association (APA) traces the beginnings of classification and diagnosis to the early days of census taking in the 1840s, when there was one category of mental illness, "idiocy/insanity." By the next census there were seven categories, and in the twentieth century APA developed a classification system, adopted by the American Medical Association's standard system of diseases.[3] With each new addition, more disorders were added. Some critics say that the increase in classifiable disorders simply allows more types of problems to be paid for by insurance, while others insist that the increase is due to the fact that more types of problems are "discovered" every year [4] (see Box 1.3).

Over time, disorders multiplied, and the APA codified diagnoses and developed the DSM in 1952, now in its fourth edition. However,

BOX 1.3
Something You Should Know

In DSM-IV there is no assumption that each category of mental disorder is a completely discrete entity with absolute boundaries dividing it from other mental disorders or from no mental disorder. There is also no assumption that all individuals described as having the same mental disorder are alike in all important ways. (*Source:* APA, 2000, p. xxxi)

the DSM is difficult to use with objectivity and accuracy for several reasons. First, diagnostic labels are just words—words that try to describe something specifically enough so that others will clearly and objectively understand it.

Most of the disorders or conditions in the DSM do not have clearly demonstrated causes.[5] Research shows that several different clinicians might diagnosis a client quite differently. Several studies demonstrated that diagnosis is not always accurate, and can be wrong.[6] However, an agreed-upon set of diagnoses is useful to help skilled and unassuming clinicians communicate with one another. But a diagnosis should never be taken as the last word on any human dilemma.

TOP TEN PROBLEMS WITH THE MEDICAL MODEL

1. The medical model attempts to find *the problem* and target it for change. This assumes that producing the correct changes in the brain will "fix" the problem. (Hence the popularity of medication.) But the concept of single causes is outdated, even in most simple biological problems, let alone psychological.[7]

   Even the common cold has multiple potential causes. Indeed, one of the most commonly known facts in mental health is that problems are overdetermined—caused by many factors arriving at the same place to create symptoms. The placebo effect, or the measurable improvement in a condition for which the client has only taken a placebo, or inert medication, demonstrates equally effective results as medication for many conditions. Furthermore, there is evidence that the physician's belief in the treatment condition, even when it is a placebo, contributes to a positive outcome in a significant number of cases.[8]

2. Medications for psychological problems often produce side effects, sometimes serious ones. Recent exposes about the dangers of giving antidepressants to children and adolescents should be warning enough. Although the drug manufacturers continue to work to find medications with fewer side effects, a review of a *Physician's Desk Reference* or a glance at the pamphlet that accompanies these medications will list the most commonly associated side effects. Read the insert of medication carefully, and talk with your physician if you have concerns. Many people suffering from debilitating psychiatric and psychological symptoms seek relief only to find that they now have a myriad of other physical problems.
3. Clinicians at different sites will experience different results with the same medications used for the same conditions. Why? Research shows that the human factor (talk therapy and relationship) has an important effect on outcome. In other words, the use of medication alone is not as effective as the combined effect of medication and counseling/psychotherapy. Research funded by the National Institute of Mental Health's (NIMH) Treatment of Depression Collaborative Research Program demonstrated that with most types of depression the interpersonal relationship and the *quality* of that relationship were important to a positive outcome. In fact, the interpersonal conditions of empathy and caring as well as the clinician's willingness to be open and sincere seemed to be the factors that pointed to positive outcomes regardless of whether the client was also being treated with medication.[9]
4. If you don't take the medication, it'll never work! Lack of medical compliance (not taking your meds) not only guarantees to make them ineffective, it can put your health at risk. Nonetheless, estimates are that about half of clients fail to follow referral advice, 75 percent miss follow-up appointments, and half with chronic illnesses drop out of treatment within one year.[10]
5. Most treatments based on the biological model focus on what's wrong, rather than on eliciting strengths, resiliencies, or wellness. Such a perspective can encourage or even force

clinicians to look for, and find, problems that may not really be problems.

6. The biological model tends to split the working of the brain from that of mind and body. Wholeness is thereby negated. This way of thinking rules out the effect of independent thinking, feelings, societal inputs, or cultural beliefs. This division has implications. If psychiatric problems are biological, then why are they called *mental* problems?
7. The insurance business, and it *is* a profit-driven business, *forces* a medically modeled perspective. It has been estimated that it costs 50 percent less to prescribe medications to treat the *symptoms* of a problem than it does for longer-term psychological counseling, even though there is overwhelming evidence that psychotherapy is the most effective treatment for many types of psychological problems. Moreover, many recent studies have shown that the use of medication without counseling is often not as effective in the long run.
8. One-on-one treatments are costly compared to prevention and do little to eradicate the causes of problems. Unlike smallpox or cholera, no major mental illness has ever been eradicated by one-on-one treatments. Numerous studies have shown that mental and emotional problems are associated with disenfranchisement and poverty. If we were to eradicate poverty and empower people, the incidence of these dilemmas would decrease.
9. According to the American Medical Association, any primary care physician (PCP) can prescribe medication for most psychological problems. This means that PCPs without adequate psychiatric training or knowledge can and do prescribe psychiatric medications. As a result of this, many people are overdiagnosed and treated for problems without adequate follow up or the proper referrals to a clinician trained in some form of psychotherapy. Granted, physicians are under a great deal of pressure to alleviate patients' suffering quickly, but if they have not been trained to understand the need for counseling as a primary or complementary part of treatment or, worse yet, hold biased positions against talk therapy in favor of medications, they can do more harm than good.

10. Recent studies have demonstrated that 56 percent of those who authored the DSM have at least one financial tie to the pharmaceutical companies, making conflicts of interest a difficult question to fess up to. All of the authors who worked on mood disorders, schizophrenia, and psychotic disorder sections of the DSM had financial ties to pharmaceutical companies for research dollars, or as a consultant or guest speaker on big pharma's payroll. One need not wonder at how the use of medications have become the treatment du jour.[1]

CONCLUSION

If the field is going to treat emotional dilemmas with medication, then these medications should probably be administered by someone trained in psychiatry. However, the average psychiatrist charges about four times as much as a PCP, so that's just not practical.

There is certainly a time and place for medication; for severe problems such as chronic depression leading to potential suicide, as well as for schizophrenic, psychotic, and bipolar syndromes, or in the beginning of some treatments in combination with counseling, chemical treatment is highly effective. However, many psychological dilemmas are easily and more appropriately treated using counseling, not medication alone (see Box 1.4).

In the next chapter we come to the psychology and counseling models of cause and treatment of mental health problems. We will begin to unveil those mysteries as well.

BOX 1.4
Something You Should Know

Psychiatric medication should be used as part of a comprehensive plan of treatment, with ongoing medical assessment and, in most cases, individual and/or family psychotherapy. (*Source:* American Academy of Child and Adolescent Psychiatry, 2004)

Chapter 2

The Psychological Models

> Kingdoms rise, and kingdoms fall, but you go on.
>
> U2 (1981)

Psychology has an interesting history, which dates back several thousands of years to Greek philosophers. Nineteenth-century psychologists moved into the laboratory to study human behavior scientifically. The emphasis was on perception, behavior, and the mind. Psychology soon splintered into various groups, all trying to understand human behavior and the mind. If we fast-forward to the late 1940s and early 1950s, one can see how psychology began to take the road more traveled.

Two events changed the focus of psychology after World War II. The Veterans Administration provided thousands of jobs for psychologists, and the National Institute of Mental Health funded grants to research mental illness for psychologists affiliated with colleges and universities. Previously, psychology was dedicated to making the

BOX 2.1
Politics of Mental Health

When therapy succeeds, the convention is to attribute the positive outcome to the therapy or ministrations of the therapist. In contrast, when therapy goes awry, or at least yields disappointing results, it has been customary to place the failure in the client or the client's personality. (*Source:* Hubble, Duncan, & Miller, 1999, p. 47) lives of all people more productive and fulfilling, as well as nurturing great talents.[1] However, at this point, instead of human potential, pathology became the primary direction of modern psychology. This change allowed psychologists to continue their professional and financial advancement on a more equal par with psychiatrists. In the twenty-first century, the same economic drive now directs energies toward empirically validated treatments (EVTs), attempting to produce valid products and stay in the game with psychiatry. EVTs are now a common requirement for reimbursement of services.[2] Some clinicians, however, call them "paint-by-numbers" therapy, yet funding sources are already mandating their use, just as they insist on medications. As psychiatry and other medical professions labor to refine medical treatments, psychology also works to find effective and specific treatments. However, this mechanistic, one-size-fits-all thinking has us believing that people are the same, and that their parts are broken or worn out. Treatment becomes medications and/or EVT therapies in most cases, instead of an individualized plan, or admittance that sometimes there are no silver bullets.[3]

Against this backdrop of history, we look at some of the models psychology has developed. From Freud's talking cure, modern-day psychology has developed theories about how problems develop, as well as treatments to fix them. Over the years, many of these models have come and gone, but for our purposes, they fit into four categories: (1) developmental, (2) behavioral, (3) humanistic, and (4) cognitive theory. Crossovers of categories with models occur, but we have placed them this way to make it easier for you to understand.

DEVELOPMENTAL THEORIES

If you have ever thought about how you have changed over time, and wondered what life might have been like if events had been different as you grew up, you are thinking about how you developed during your life. *Developmental* theories assume that people go through specific stages, one after another. Problems are believed to be the result of breaks or difficulties during development, and/or being stuck at one level. Problems, according to this model, are due to a lack of growth to the next stage. Change occurs only if the person is able to move and grow past the stage where he or she is stuck.

Freud's psychosexual developmental theory maintains that people go through several stages of development from birth to early childhood, and that much of what happens is instinctual. You are therefore limited in choice and free will.

Freud believed that most of the stimulation one received during infancy and toddler development was *early* erotic sexual feelings. This is not to be confused with adult sexuality or eroticism, but he clearly believed the stimulation was pleasurable, thus erotic. The stages are: (a) the *oral stage* during infancy when the child learns about her or his world from the contact and *attachment* with an adult caretaker during feeding; (b) the *anal stage* when a toddler derives pleasure (eros) from evacuation and control of his or her bowels, learning *mastery,* and (c) the *phallic stage* during a child's third or fourth year, when the erogenous zone moves to the genitalia. Accordingly, it is at this stage that the Oedipus (for boys) and Electra (for girls) complexes come into play, with the child wanting to have a personal and exclusive relationship with the parent of the opposite sex. Freud attached special significance to the resolution of this stage with respect to growth and behavior.

The *latency stage,* usually thought to occur between ages six and twelve, is a time when socialization occurs, and any unworked issues from the earlier stages may be reworked. Children who are troubled at this point of life can trace their problems back to unresolved development during earlier stages. There is much more to his psychodynamic theory, but Freud bases the causes of most psychological problems on the unmet needs during early development.

Much of later psychological thought is based on either adaptations to, or attempts to move far away from, this way of thinking. The psychodynamic model split into several different models, namely Jungian (Carl Jung), Adlerian (Alfred Adler), and the Psychosynthesis of Assagioli, and later, neo-Freudian (as with Karen Horney), each with its own view of how people develop, grow, and become symptomatic. Each of these new psychodynamic theories removed or reworked the importance that Freud placed on sexuality, and replaced it with what they believed to be important. But Freudian psychodynamic language remains with us, not only as a remnant, but as a basis of how we think, talk about, and use words to describe what takes place during therapy. Words like *neurotic, id, ego, superego, transference,* and *termination* are from Freud's theories. Today you are more likely to hear these ideas used in literature and the media rather than in psychology. Freudian concepts have become a part of our culture.

Psychologist Abraham Maslow came up with a simple and elegant model of human development which proposes that for people to thrive they need to move through a *hierarchy of basic needs*. Maslow expressed a way of understanding how people move developmentally to higher levels of being, with the goal being self-sufficiency and even self-actualization. Moving through these needs occurs as one interacts with the environment, and lower needs are satisfied. The needs are (1) basic physical requirements, (2) safety and security, (3) love and belonging, and (4) esteem needs. Maslow sees all these needs as essential. When lower needs are unmet, you cannot devote yourself to fulfilling your potential. Maslow's final stage is self-actualization in which one is responsible for and responsive to her or his own destiny, happiness, and welfare (see Box 2.2).

Maslow's theory correlates well with what public health professionals tell us about the incidence and distribution of mental illness. In areas where there is marked poverty, social isolation, and alienation, people seem to have higher rates of health problems of all kinds. The biological conditions believed related to syndromes with which people are diagnosed may not be biological at all but related to conditions of disempowerment and disenfranchisement from the mainstream group.[4,5]

Maslow's Hierarchy: Rate Yourself

Using Maslow's Hierarchy of Needs (as we lumped them here), rate yourself on a scale from 1 (low) to 5 (high) on the following:

BOX 2.2
Something You Should Know

What a man can be, he must be. This is the need we may call self-actualization . . . It refers to man's desire for fulfillment, namely to the tendency for him to become actually in what he is potentially: to become everything that one is capable of becoming . . . (*Source:* Maslow, 2000, p. 1)

- *Physiological needs.* Do you have a roof over your head, nutritious food to eat, and clothes appropriate to your environment and comfort?
- *Safety and security needs.* Do you feel fairly safe in your environment, not threatened on a daily or continual basis, and free to move about with relative ease?
- *Need for love and belonging.* Do you feel that you belong in the group or groups you interact with, and that people care and love you?
- *Esteem needs.* On a day to day basis do you feel good about yourself and what you are doing, and that others in your environments feel you are worthwhile and useful to them also?

If you can rate yourself in the 4 to 5 range within each category, and feel that ratings lower than that are transitory and will soon come back into the higher ranges, then you are probably doing okay.

BEHAVIORAL THEORY

Behavioral psychology, or *behaviorism,* was developed by John Watson (1878-1958) in the late 1800s. If you have ever offered your children a few bucks to mow the lawn, given them a piece of candy to be quiet while taking a long trip, or even bartered with yourself by eating a salad so that you could attain your weight loss goal, you have been working a behavioral program. Behaviorists insist that psychology is the science of behavior, not mind, and that it is possible to explain behavior without understanding mental events. A behaviorist's explanation of problems is that they are habitual behavior patterns that can be changed. In order to fix them one does not need to know how or why people think or feel, only what can be done to change the habitual patterns. As dogs are taught to behave in certain ways (lie down, roll over) in order to receive a reward, humans are conditioned or taught and retaught to change their behavior. Mind is taken out of the equation. Feelings, thoughts, beliefs, and cultural conditions have little or no part in the end result within a behavioral framework. Basically, it boils down to someone else (clinician, teacher, etc.) designing a program for attaining a change or desired change for you. By conditioning or reinforcing and shaping targeted and desired behavior with positive rewards and stimulation, behavior is acted upon, changed, and reinforced. The behavioral model works very well for many problem conditions such as phobias, unwanted fears, learning problems, and other unwanted behavior.

Token economies and delayed rewards for target behavior, i.e., turning in homework, increasing work productivity, or changes in harmful behaviors through reinforcement of new, more productive behaviors are examples of behavioral therapy.

A Learning Tale

I (Jeff) was beginning a swimming-for-exercise program at the college where I first taught. I noticed a man come into the locker room, open the locker, take his shoes off, put them in the locker, and then put them back on and leave. The next day, he did the same thing, except that this time his socks came off, and then he put them back on again. Strange, I thought. Slowly, over time, he got to the point where he had changed into his swimsuit, and slowly—painfully slow—he inched his way into the pool area. Over weeks, he finally sat on the side of the pool and put his feet, and then his legs into the pool.

When I finally got up the nerve to ask what he was doing (I didn't want to embarrass him), he told me that he had a fear of water, and at age forty wanted to get over it. His therapist had designed this delightful, safe, albeit slow, behavioral program to get him close to, and finally into the water.

Behavioral therapy has proven useful in many such human dilemmas. Behaviors or even emotions that keep people from living fuller lives are extinguished and changed. From all-too-common phobias and fears, as an adjunct to defeating depression and oppositional behavior, to unwanted conditions like poor learning habits, behavioral therapy is an effective, fairly quick and useful treatment that should be considered.

HUMANISTIC THEORY

The third wave of psychology—*humanism*—came about during the late 1950s and early 1960s as a direct response to behaviorists and psychoanalysts, who, it was believed, had taken the soul out of therapy with their focus on instincts and negative views of humans by psychoanalysis, and input/output, and manipulation of people through behaviorism. Based on the existential humanistic philosophies, this view concerns itself with how humans create meaning, make choices, develop, and use relationships in life. Humanists believe in the innate good nature of humans to move toward health in their lives, and they believe dilemmas happen when a person is not in tune with his or her true inner nature. Humanists work with choices, relationships, and feelings.

Prominent humanistic psychologist, Carl Rogers's views are some of the most widely held in the field today. Rogers believes that people are, at their core, basically good or healthy—not bad or ill. He viewed mental "health" as the normal progression of life toward higher, more fulfilling involvement, and human problems as being distortions of that natural tendency. According to Rogers, as humans go about their lives, they struggle with the difference between being regarded positively by others, either with *conditional* positive regard, or unconditional positive regard. For instance, choosing to stay after work so that the boss will be pleased, even at the risk of forsaking what you had planned would elicit *conditional regard,* while a mother's love would/might be *unconditional.* Think about how your own life has been shaped because you wanted to please others, and modified your own behavior or feelings to win their approval.

Humanists developed models that help people work with their feelings, become "real" and congruent in their lives, and make choices that will affect their growth toward being better people. Humanists work with people's potential.

Humanists view a helping relationship (clinician plus client) as helping people grow by recognizing their authentic feelings. As people become aware of their feelings, making choices and behaving congruently, healing takes place. This happens when the clinician has unconditional positive regard for the client as a person, is empathic, and is genuine (not phony). These factors, called the "necessary and sufficient conditions" of therapy, which are fundamental to the success of all forms of therapy, including the prescribing of medication. These conditions create a working alliance or "therapeutic relationship" between the client and the clinician. The use of these "conditions," no matter what model is used, are linked to a positive outcome in therapy.[6]

A Learning Tale

Think you are always aware of what you are feeling, and act congruently? Well, so did one of my students. Lisa was the youngest of four siblings, born into a family that had prohibitions against saying what was really on an individual's mind. As Lisa grew up, she and her older brother grew distant until they were not speaking, except in anger. Lisa's brother, Thomas, had joined a fundamentalist church, and didn't approve of some of Lisa's behavior. Thomas would get upset with Lisa for the clothing she wore, men she dated, and for not remaining at home with her parents even though she was twenty-eight-years old. Their discussions would get heated, and angry exchanges always ended in them parting company with Lisa feeling unheard, misunderstood, and belittled.

During one class period, she volunteered to talk about a family conflict, and as we role-played, I asked her what she was feeling. She said, "I'm really pissed off because he always puts me down." I said, "What do you tell him about how you are feeling?" Again, she said she told him how angry she was. I countered with a new perspective, "What else are you feeling? Are you sad, too?" With this she began to cry, and I stopped the role-play so she could gain composure. But the point had been made. Anger was covering up her sadness. Rather than being vulnerable with her real feelings, Lisa had covered them up, as most of us do, with anger and hostility. When she was able to tell Thomas how she really felt, without the anger, he softened. They began to work at listening and being with each other again.

Learning Theories

Cognitive therapies are some of the most researched models of psychology. If you have ever told yourself over and over again, "you can do this," or if you have checked your thoughts to see if they are rational or not, or read affirmations so that you will not become unnerved with thoughts about yourself, you have used cognitive therapy. These are associated with some of the earliest forms of psychological studies—*theories of the mind.* These theories suggest that people create psychological problems for themselves, and make changes, through what happens in their minds (see Box 2.3).

Mind is much more than the chemical processes in your brain, or conditional responses. Mind is a whole filtering process that includes what one has learned over time from one's family, culture, education,

BOX 2.3
Something You Should Know

Research on neural nets indicated that the brain doesn't process images of the world literally, like a camera, but rather registers experiences in patterns organized by the nervous system of the observer. Nothing is perceived directly. Everything is filtered through the mind of the observer. (*Source:* Nichol & Schwartz, 2001, p. 60) the environment, as well as how one has captured and made that learning one's own. Cognitive therapy is the restructuring of, or relearning in the mind.

Some of the most important contributions to the field of mind are the *social learning theory* of Albert Bandura, and the *cognitive behavioral theories* and therapies of psychologist Albert Ellis (rational emotive behavioral therapy) and psychiatrist Aaron T. Beck. One newcomer (term) to the field, *positive psychology,* is a unique addition to the others. For now, however, let us briefly look at the work of Bandura.

Albert Bandura, a social psychologist, studied how people learn from their social environment. He pioneered self-efficacy, which is the knowledge one has about their own ability to learn, accomplish, and be successful in life. Self-efficacy happens, in varying degrees, when a person learns about himself or herself from the environment. You learn about your abilities, and significant behaviors, through interactions with others, and through modeling what you observe. Bandura found that children who have observed violence display those same behaviors more frequently than children who have not. In addition, he found that people believe in their ability to succeed because they have been taught they can succeed.

Cognitive therapies, originally conceived by Albert Ellis (Rational Emotive Therapy-RET) and Aaron T. Beck (Cognitive Behavioral Therapy-CBT), contend that it is mistaken thinking that causes problems. Distorted pictures of events in your life and about yourself cause anxiety, depression, or anger. Changing your thinking, for instance through daily affirmations, can change the way you think and behave. An example of an unhealthy thought would be: "hard work will *always* pay off," or "it is important that everyone always like me," even though there is no evidence that you must behave that way to be a good or successful person, or have a better life. Living up to these thoughts and expectations can lead to problems, so cognitive therapy attempts to help people dispute and change them. Both Ellis and Beck and their followers have specific protocols to help people change the way they think.

Cognitive therapies are some of the most successful means of changing thoughts and behaviors. CBT is highly successful in working with depression, phobias, and anxiety disorders. CBT has become one of the empirically validated treatments (EVTs) we talked about earlier,

BOX 2.4
Something You Should Know

I do not believe that you should devote overly much effort to correcting your weaknesses. Rather, I believe that the highest success in living and the deepest emotional satisfaction comes from building and using your signature strengths. (*Source:* Seligman, 2002, p. xxx)

and may be required by an insurance company as a method of treatment for specific problems regardless of the circumstances.

Positive psychology, one of the most unique and relevant models to come from psychology, is the brainchild of former APA President Martin Seligman.[7] Concerned that psychology had abandoned its original purpose, Seligman began a study of factors that protect and drive people to wellness and better living. Positive psychology helps people address their "signature strengths" and downplay their deficits. You can take one of his tests, either in Seligman's well-written and intriguing book, *Authentic Happiness,* or online at: http://www.authentichappiness.org/. Positive psychology is a breath of fresh air in a field of muck and mire. This model is helping move the field away from pathologizing, toward collaboration and strengths, possibilities and resiliency. It is at least a helpful addition to a search for wholeness, and, at best, a method that will transform you (see Box 2.4).

This completes our look at the basic psychological models and how they understand and believe in treating human dilemmas.

Now, let's examine a few of the most common problems associated with all of the psychologically oriented models more closely.

TOP FIVE PROBLEMS WITH A PSYCHOLOGICAL MODEL

1. Psychology continues to find many views of "causes" for mental health concerns. No one unified view exists and they almost all seem to default to the use of DSM categories.
2. Development is not always continuous. Stage theory misses this concept sometimes, believing one must go through each stage.
3. Psychology maintains a pathological stance despite leaders in the field offering reasonable alternatives. Strength-based, resiliency, and positive psychology models offer useful alternatives.

4. Although most research repeatedly shows that the most important qualities in therapy have to do with relationship, and that techniques are limited to only around 15 percent of outcome, psychology still looks for the holy grail of EVTs.
5. The focus of treatment on "after-the-fact," costly, one-on-one treatment rather than providing prevention programs is shortsighted. Public health models have demonstrated the efficacy of prevention over treatment as a cost-effective model. However, some believe this would be hazardous to clinicians' financial success.

CONCLUSION

Psychological models have shown repeatedly the advantage of treating mental health concerns within the context of a relationship. Research has shown that talking cures are effective for several concerns currently classified as psychiatric.[8] Problems such as anxiety, panic attacks, depression, post-traumatic stress, phobias, and obsessions, to name a few, commonly treated with medication by well-meaning general practitioners, respond equally well to psychological treatments without the chance of side effects. Many problems may be treated with multimodal models including family treatment, changes in life style, alternative medicine, and a comprehensive plan that will provide the best bang for the long-term buck.

Chapter 3 discusses the last of our models: the family systems model. In this chapter we will see a model that some believe to be very important, while others push it aside believing it places undo blame on families and not enough emphasis on the chemicals in one's brain.

Chapter 3

The Systems Models

> The field of mental health has long neglected the study and promotion of health. In the concentration on mental illness, family normality became equated with the absence of symptoms, a situation rarely, if ever, seen in the clinical setting.
>
> Froma Walsh (2003, p. 27)

The last of the models of causes and treatments of human dilemmas are the family systems models. These models, begun in the middle 1940s, look for explanations for dilemmas within the family unit. Family systems models explore the "nurture" model of human dilemmas. Clinicians who use a systems model believe dilemmas need to be examined and treated in context. In the early 1950s, clinicians who were willing to break with the existing psychodynamic and biological traditions, were enchanted by the newer systems model. They began to borrow ideas from the sciences of systems theory and quantum physics. Believing systems concepts provided a clearer, more complete view of human dilemmas, early clinicians worked with the families of their clients.

WHAT IS A SYSTEM?

A system is a series of interrelated, interdependent, interconnected parts whose whole is greater than the sum of its parts. Systems are not linear, with the usual "cause and effect" explanations of traditional science, but involve multiple causations as well as recursive (reacting back on that which began that process) causation. All people are interconnected, and so what you do to others comes back to affect yourself. And like the common cold, there is never only one cause of a problem, but many contributing factors that come together in a unique way to create the illness.

Traditional analysis focuses on separating the individual pieces of what is being studied; in fact, the word "analysis" actually comes from the root meaning "to break into constituent parts." Systems thinking, in contrast, focuses on interactions between the parts of the system—the relationships that produce behavior. Instead of isolating smaller and smaller parts of the system to look for the problem, family systems clinicians expand their view to take into account larger and larger interactions. This results in strikingly different conclusions than those generated by traditional forms of analysis, especially when the family system being treated is dynamic, complex, or has a great deal of feedback from other sources.

Early family therapists called clients "symptom bearers" or "identified patient," indicating that the problem was within the family system, not within the person. Symptoms are seen as attempts to change current rigid family patterns. For instance, an acting-out child could be seen as providing "information" that the system is too rigid, or as a distractor for a failing marriage. Symptoms are not evidence of dysfunctional *people* but rather a call for change. In fact, the term "dysfunctional family system" was intended to indicate that the *family patterns* were problematic, not people.

Early family systems models looked at how certain behaviors and perceptions (worldviews) pass from generation to generation.[1] Calling this "intergenerational transmission," clinicians used genograms—family trees indicating family lineage as well as behavioral and emotional patterns—to document the cascading problems as they pass from one generation to the next. Family violence, child rearing, all manner of beliefs and behaviors are passed from one generation to the next. We are largely, like it or not, products of our parents', grandparents', and great-great grandparents' beliefs and behaviors, passed down the generational line. From this point of view, problems do not reside "inside" humans, but are the result of interactions and patterns within family systems.

Family systems models evolved and changed over the decades, from blaming families, to finally working with them as equal stakeholders. Yet, the National Alliance for the Mentally Ill (NAMI) did not find the family systems stance helpful at all. Some felt blamed for their family members' mental illness, and so they worked hard to ensure that biology was considered the "real" cause of *all* mental health concerns. Biomedical health care was more than glad to take up the cause, and family systems concepts were under attack (see Box 3.2).

But few could dispute the affect of family on client progress. Soon, family therapy became integrated into practice by almost every mental health profession, some with good training, and others with sketchy training. Family systems therapy was beginning to be seen as a technique one could use with little or no training, rather than as a way to view problem formation and treatment.

Many well-trained family clinicians use family systems models, and have excellent success with their clients. In fact, family systems models are more effective than traditional methods when treating adult alcoholism, adolescent drug abuse, helping families keep a schizophrenic member in a state of remission, women with depression, families with oppositional-defiant children, troubled marriages, and much more.[2]

The most frequently used models today are Murray Bowen's *Systems Therapy,* Salvador Minuchin's *Structural Therapy,* and the Post-

BOX 3.1
Something You Should Know

All [family therapy] models view flexibility as essential to healthy family functioning. (*Source:* Walsh, 2003, p. 40)

BOX 3.2
Something You Should Know

In their zeal to rescue family "scapegoats" from the clutches of their "pathological families," early family therapists provoked some of the resistance they complained of. Therapists who think of themselves as rescuing innocent victims from their families and who take an adversarial stance are not unlike the person who whacks a turtle on the back and them complains that the creature doesn't want to come out of its shell. (*Source:* Nichol & Schwartz, 2006, p. 28)

modern influenced models of Steve deShazar and Insoo Kim Berg's *Solution-Focused Therapy,* and Michael White and David Epston's *Narrative Therapy.* We will briefly look at each of these models to understand their premises about what they see as causing problems, as well as their clinical applications.

BOWEN FAMILY SYSTEMS THEORY

Psychiatrist Murray Bowen focused on intergenerational transmission of problems. One of the first to articulate that family patterns can cause present-day dilemmas, Bowen did not mean that immediate family is always to blame for concerns, but that problems can be maintained by patterns and beliefs that span generations.[3]

Patterns, such as child-rearing practices, beliefs about relationships, religion, personal rights and responsibilities, if the world is a safe or fearful place, and how you deal with emotions, are all related to family rules passed down through generations.

One of the behavior patterns, "triangulation," occurs when you are angry with a family member and complain about it to another. Bowen believed that rather than complaining and vilifying who you are angry at behind his or her back, it is better to discuss it with the person face to face, and work out or express your feelings directly. Triangulation is a central contributor to problems, according to Bowen. He believed that people need to move past the strong anxiety, reactivity, and subtle pulls families have on us, to a position where discussing differences of opinions and strong emotions with family members in a calm and rational manner can take place without using triangles.

Bowen believed that the ability to disagree with others, and hold one's own position without anger or reactivity, was what is known as "differentiated." By being clear about differences of opinion, and accepting others' views and differences as just that—differences—maturity would allow for growth personally and in the family. To be differentiated, he argued, you must not let your anger get the best of you, but maturely hold your ground, adult to adult. Difficult? Very.

A Teaching Vignette

It was my freshman year in college (Jeff); spring break was coming at me fast. I told an older friend that I was worried about going home, because my parents would not like some of the new ideas I had, or ideologies I was beginning to assimilate (this was the middle 1960s, and Vietnam and the government were topics of controversy at our house). My friend said "just tell them you are sorry that they do not agree with you, but you have a different perspective now. Tell them that you are growing up and that means that you might have some differences with them about the world."

It seemed so simple, but I thought that they would off-handedly put me down for my new-found voice. I was surprised that when I said those magic words, it stopped them in their tracks, and made them think. It saved a lot of angry, hot arguments. I was doing Bowen's therapy before I even knew what it was, as well as starting a slow process of becoming my own person.

So, according to Bowen's family systems model, several points can be made: (1) differentiation is an ongoing lifelong process, but it is also what makes us more mature, and mentally and emotionally healthy; (2) running or moving away from your family so you don't have to deal with them is not likely a healthy thing to do. You carry their worldview and messages in your head anyway, so it is better to work things out, and become more mature in the process. (3) Being clear about your own beliefs and being your own person in the face of opposition, with little or no reactivity is healthier than avoiding or running from the problem; (4) you should be free to be as similar to, and/or different from your family of origin *as you wish*. Our families teach us both useful and not so useful ideas about life. Choosing what is best for you may mean running counter to how you were taught by your family. (5) Triangulation is not a good way of dealing with disagreements with family or others. It is better to deal directly with those with whom you have disagreements, being as nonreactive as possible. Speak from your heart, be respectful, and ask for respect in return. Bad mouthing another person never fixes the problem, but delays your maturity and postpones honest discussion.

What Is Differentiation?

> Differentiation is a lifelong process of striving to keep one's being in balance through the reciprocal external and internal processes of self-definition and self-regulation. It is a concept that can be difficult to focus on objectively. It means to have the capacity to become one's self out of one's self with minimum reactivity to the positions or reactions of others. It is charting one's own way by means of one's own internal guidance system

> rather than perpetually eyeing the scope of others. It means to be able to take a stand in an intense emotional system and to say "I" when others are demanding that you say "we." It means being clear about one's own personal goals, values and ideas, and taking personal responsibility for one's own reactions and emotional being. It means not blaming others for one's own emotional being and for one's own destiny rather than blaming it on others, i.e., one's parents, race or culture or gender or set of circumstances. (Bowen, 1974)[4]

STRUCTURAL FAMILY THERAPY

Psychiatrist Salvador Minuchin developed structural family therapy while consulting at a residential treatment program for children. He noticed that the children he worked with were in control of their family, rather than the parent(s). The children's behaviors were so severe that the parents were unable to get them under control. Convinced that these types of problems were created when family structures become misaligned, and when unwritten rules of the family were unbalanced or structurally flawed, Minuchin set out to find methods by which he could realign them (see Box 3.3).

Structural family therapy is a pragmatic, problem-solving therapy that works to realign hierarchies that exist in family systems by helping parents get back in charge of their children. Structural family therapy is goal oriented, and attempts to help families get back on

BOX 3.3
Something You Should Know

Structure is the organized patterns and predictable sequences in an organization. These patterns become family rules that exist in unmentioned, covert family operating principles.

Hierarchy consists of both a soft side that is responsible for nurturing and care, and a hard side that consists of rule making and enforcement. When parents do not work together because one is hard and the other is soft, they do not complement each other, but tend to cancel each other out. For an organization (family) to operate effectively, both sides need to be present and work together.

track. Problems ranging from oppositional defiant disorder to anorexia and bulimia have been treated using structural family therapy. Structural family therapy was one of the most widely used forms of therapy during the 1970s and 1980s because the model can be learned quickly and usually produces dramatic results rapidly.

Structural therapy looks for boundaries that are either too rigid, or too loose, with the belief that families are on a relational continuum ranging from enmeshment to disengagement. Families who are enmeshed value and enforce closeness within the family, know everyone's business, and have caretakers who take care of children past the point of being useful. Enmeshed families believe that the family is central, and individuals are secondary.

On the other end of the continuum are families who are disengaged, spend little time together, do not support one another during times of need, with children who fend for themselves and parents who spend little time with each other. Disengaged families reinforce the individuals' centrality over the family as primary.

Family therapists do not believe that problems are "caused" by one person, but rather happen in relationships and over time. So, as "junior" becomes more dominant in the family, parents imperceptibly let go of their authority. Families' patterns seem "normal" to them even if they are not producing happy conditions for all members.

Structural family therapy works by empowering parents to take responsibility when their children are trying to push them around. Structural therapy looks for groupings, such as parent/child coalitions that subtly undermine adult-to-adult co-parenting. The focus of structural therapy is on the present, and works to actively change the dysfunctional patterns and structures of the family system. Structural family therapy is usually a short- to moderate-term therapy.

Structural Therapy Is Useful

Structural family therapy is extremely useful for families experiencing stress with oppositional children, or when one spouse is having problems with substance abuse. In fact, when comparing outcomes, structural therapy increases the likelihood of completing a therapy regime in a substance abuse treatment center by anywhere from 64 to 94 percent, while the use of a traditional twelve-step treatment in combination with, for example, Alanon (spouse/partner support group), has a significantly lower rate of completion. In addition, when family therapy is used, 94 percent of families who attend the first session remain committed to their spouses' treatment, while those who participate with traditional treatments stayed together only 31 percent.[5,6]

POSTMODERN THERAPY

Somewhere during the late 1980s, a fresh view of family therapy specifically, and mental health in general came along. Influenced by the many academic fields that were embracing a move away from a modernist perspective to that of postmodernism, the concepts of truth, and a hierarchical relationship with one's clients went sailing out the window. Instead, language and collaboration became the important concepts. Could it be that how we talk about a problem was what caused it? And if this were so, why should only clinicians have the answers about how to change? So, gone were the days when clinicians had the correct view of her or his clients' problems. In came the *co-construction* of new ways for clients' involvement in their own treatment.

SOLUTION-FOCUSED THERAPY

Solution-focused therapy (SFT) is the product of social worker Steve deShazar and his family therapist wife, Insoo Kim Berg. The solution focused model puts the client in the expert position, rather than the clinician, strives for a collaborative relationship, and sees problems as opportunities and possibilities for new ways of living. As part of this therapy protocol, Berg and deShazar turned the usual problem-focus (the medical model) of therapy around, and began helping their clients look for solutions. By looking for exceptions to when the problem occurs, and encouraging the client to do more of that, they build solutions, by utilizing what clients are doing already. (Note: a problem focus suggests that a pathology or dysfunction is present, while a solution focus suggests that resources and personal capabilities are present.) Solution-focused therapy asks clients to search for those times when the problem isn't a problem, and then asks them to continue to do more of that (see Box 3.4).

BOX 3.4
Something You Should Know

Solution-focused therapists and authors Jane Peller and John Walters recall the time when Chicago Cubs manager Jim Fry was approached by a pitcher in a slump. He told Fry that he was going to go home and look at tapes of himself when he was pitching poorly, in order to correct his problem. Fry replied that he wanted him to only watch tapes of his pitching when he was pitching well. He did not want him to watch his poor performances, only his good ones. Makes sense! (*Source:* Walter & Peller, 1992, p. 5)

Research indicates that SFT has a positive outcome as a longer-term problem-focused therapy. Solution focused therapy is brief, simple, and positively oriented. It works well for a myriad of dilemmas where clients cannot seem to find their own way out. Rather than looking for what is wrong and how you got "damaged," solution-oriented work looks for the possibilities in life.

Something to Try

Here is an experiential exercise you can try that demonstrates the solution orientation. Solution-oriented therapist and King of Possibilities, Bill O'Hanlon suggests the following.

> *A Solution-Oriented Spirituality*
>
> *Revisit a spiritual moment or time.* Recall a time or phase in your life when you felt free, flowing, alive, energetic, expansive or resourceful.
>
> *Recreate the experience.* How did you feel in your body during that moment or those times? What was your thinking at that moment or those times? How did you relate to others during that moment or those times? What actions did you take that were different from your usual actions during that moment or those times?
>
> *Bring that sense of spirituality to any situation in which you are having current difficulty or anticipate having difficulty in the fu-*

ture. After recreating the spiritual experience, bring it to any current or future situation in which you have felt stuck, petty, selfish, or frightened. Imagine in detail how you would feel in your body and what your thinking, actions, and ways of relating to others would be from that more expansive, spiritual place. (Bill O'Hanlon, personal communication, August 4, 2004)

NARRATIVE THERAPY

Narrative therapy, one of the currently dominant models of family therapy, was invented by Australian social worker Michael White. It puts forth the idea that that people are not the problem, the problem is the problem.[7] Narrative ideas demonstrate how language constructs how we understand the world. Dominant discourse (politically correct or current beliefs) compels us to understand reality in one dimension, blocking out other possibilities. For the narrative clinician, collaborative work is one of the first keys to success. Believing that people's problems are created by the stories that they tell themselves, and others perpetuate by retelling them, problems can be saturated with negative connotations. These "problem saturated stories" keep the problem alive.

Any grade-school teacher can tell stories about students who come into their new class in September with reputations for being "troublesome," who turn out not nearly as horrible as had been described. What kept the child "a problem" were the written and unwritten stories passed on from one teacher to the next. Your stories about yourself (or about others) can keep you and others believing and acting in negative ways. And sometimes, because the story is so well developed, it seems as if there is no way out.

Narrative therapy works hard to find instances in people's stories where there are not only exceptions to the problem but examples where they find "sparkling moments" when they "defeat" the problem for a time. They then begin taking control of the problem, making it subservient rather than in charge.

Narrative therapy deconstructs (takes apart) the current story, and re-stories it from a more positive position. One method White used early on for the treatment of children with a bed-wetting problem had the therapist and client "externalizing the problem" in order to gain control over it. In this unique and playful model, children are told that "sneaky pee or sneaky poo" has "caused" them to soil the bed. The therapist then helps them to find ways they can defeat "sneaky poo or sneaky pee." White calls the soiling behavior a "vicious cycle" because the soiling causes conscious or unconscious negative feelings and behavior for both the parent and child that leads to anxiety, and then more soiling.[8] The externalization places the problem outside of the person so that he or she can gain control over it. In this way the vicious cycle is halted, and a victorious cycle begun. The child is not a "bed-wetter," but bed wetting is the problem. People are not the problem, the problem is the problem.

Something to Try

To demonstrate how language and narrative therapists work, let's try an experiment. Narrative therapist and author Jill Freedman presents this simple yet elegant way of challenging the language we use as proof of the potential for change

> Pick a character trait, quality or emotion that you feel you have too much of or that other people sometimes complain about in you. Make sure it is in adjective form, as a description of you, for instance, "angry," "competitive," "guilty," or "nitpicky." In the following set of questions, fill in the trait or emotion where we have an "X." As you read these questions, substituting the trait or emotion for X, answer them to yourself.
>
> How did you become X?
>
> What are you most X about?
>
> What kind of things happen that typically lead to your being X?
>
> When you are X, what do you do that you wouldn't do if you weren't X?
>
> What are the consequences for your life and relationships of being X?
>
> Which of your current difficulties come from being X?

How is your self-image different when you are X?

If by some miracle you woke some morning and you were not X anymore, how, specifically, would your life be different?

Note the overall effect of answering these questions. How do you feel? What seems possible in regards to this trait or emotion? What seems impossible? How does the future look in regards to this?

Now, let go of what you have just been doing. Take the same quality or trait that you worked with above and make it into a noun. For example, if "X" was "competitive, it would now become "competition;" "angry" would become "anger." In the following questions, where we've written a "Y," fill in your noun. Answer each of these questions to yourself.

What made you vulnerable to the Y so that it was able to dominate your life?

In what contexts is the Y most likely to take over?

What kinds of things happen that typically lead to the Y taking over?

What has the Y gotten you to do that is against your better judgment?

What effect does the Y have on your life and relationships?

How has the Y led you into the difficulties you are now experiencing?

Does the Y blind you from noticing your resources or can you see them through it?

Have there been times when you have been able to get the best of the Y? Times when the Y could have taken over but you kept it out of the picture?

(Freedman & Combs, 1996, pp. 49-50)[9]

Notice how your perspective on your "problem" changes as you "talk" about it differently. Narrative therapy helps people restory their lives from a problem-saturated to an open-space position where their uniqueness can shine. Narrative family therapy is the last in this series of systems models.

Now, let's examine more closely a few of the most common problems associated with the systems model.

TOP SIX PROBLEMS WITH A FAMILY SYSTEMS MODEL

1. As has happened with the other models, the science has changed over time, leaving a feeling of incompleteness. With all the different models, what is the "correct" reason for dilemmas and the proper treatment for them?
2. Even though the different models of family systems have evolved and no longer blame family members, the reality is that families do feel at fault, or blame the member, or totally reject the notion that they have any influence or accountability for the dilemma.
3. Insurance companies and managed care have yet to figure out how to bill correctly for family treatment. In some models, "family therapy" can be completed with only one person present, while at other times members of the family are seen as collateral but useful additions to treatment. Because each contact needs to be coded, and the system only pays for interviews with individuals with "treatable diseases," payment issues abound.
4. The issue of an "identified patient" creates an ethical dilemma for the clinician who must provide a diagnostic code for an individual.
5. There is no guarantee that a clinician practicing family therapy has adequate training in systems therapy.
6. As with all of the previous models, there are clinicians who believe this model is the best for all problems. Clinicians learn a model and usually stick to it. However, many psychological issues respond well to the other models, and some respond best to a concerted effort involving biology, psychology, and family treatment, in complement.

CONCLUSION

In this chapter's discussion of the various models of mental health/illness and treatment, we moved from a biological disease model, which looks for the cause of problems *within* the individual person that can be corrected with medications, to psychological models, which identifies problems in the way the mind or brain work and the corresponding "talk" therapies. Finally, we discussed family systems models that look at how an individual is impacted by his or her family. Problems can be understand as biological abnormalities that need fixing, psychological abnormalities that are created within the individual by outside forces, or family systemic problems that are created in contexts.

One of the problems plaguing the mental health field is that it does not have a vehicle to coordinate the efforts, bring all the views together in a comprehensive manner, and give credit to each with respect to whatever problem a client presents. Each clinician is trained, as we shall see in the next chapter, with a particular understanding of how problems are created, and thus, how to treat them. Einstein was right when he said "our theories determine what we see."

Words formulate how we think about something, and are compounded by the power of an authority pronouncing its version of truth. These words may keep us embedded in problems. Words can create contexts for change. Words and the way we think about an event can change drastically. Words of hope, healing, and collaboration can unlock problems we once saw as overwhelming. And words can create blocks.

To better understand this, let's look at a vignette.

A Teaching Vignette

The grandmother of one of my best friends lost her husband of fifty years. She had never driven a car, written a check, paid a bill, or done a hundred other things that most people take for granted. She went into a deep sadness or depression (look carefully at the two words—sadness and depression—and how the choice of which to use can affect what we think). She began to act strange, and her three adult children began to worry about her, expressing concerns about who would be responsible for her care. She cried a lot, lost interest in housekeeping, and was noncommunicative with family except to say strange things. She became upset and hard on her children; she appeared to be a scared woman alone for the first time; she told her children the devil was in her kitchen. Hearing these distressing words, the family sought help. A psychiatrist saw the woman, and hearing about her words and radical changes, diagnosed her with schizophrenia, prescribed medication, and had her hospitalized.

Now, the power of that word *schizophrenia* had tremendous effects. First, the family was relieved, then scared, and later worried. What does it mean to have a "schizophrenic" family member? Who will take care of her? Will she be like this forever? Will we catch it or become like her? Is it genetic? A flood of thoughts and worries came into their heads.

Several years after the hospitalization, I met my friend's grandma at a family event. She was gracious, kind, loving of her grandchildren, and very glad to meet one of her grandchild's friends. She was not acting strange, no longer used medication, and showed no signs of being schizophrenic. In my clinical opinion, she was not schizophrenic—not like those I worked with at the state hospital where I first practiced. Depression, extreme sadness, and loneliness can do very weird things to a person and I believe this woman was acting strange out of her deep grief. But her daughter and son-in-law still seemed caught up in the web of the word schizophrenia. I think they felt validated and relieved by a diagnosis. It gave them comfort to have a name for her problem, and a plan for dealing with it. The tragedy, from my perspective, is not that she was mentally ill—I don't believe she was—but that someone had pathologized grief.

Diagnoses become powerful words that we believe to be "true" almost all the time. Diagnoses shape the way we *feel* and *act* toward others, even those in our own families. These words cause us to believe and see the worst as a possible outcome, when it may not be. This is what happened to my friend's grandmother, who was viewed by most of her family as a "problem" that had to be dealt with, rather than a sad woman who would probably come out of her grief over time with understanding and love.

The field of mental health has evolved over the past several decades. The mental health profession, with its many views, is imbedded in a cultural and professional bias that is directed toward "quick fixes" and better "bottom lines," focusing on pathology rather than resiliency and strengths. The differences in the models can be confusing. However, armed with knowledge about of each model, its beliefs and methods, you will be that much wiser in choosing which model might be most helpful and least problematic for you.

Mental health is at a crossroad. Gone are the days when health care—mental health care—was a profession that attracted groups of individuals who held purly altruistic values. Today, it is a system burdened by half truths, a plethora of models that don't work together, and a capitalistic mentality. Clinicians' fees have escalated out of control for services that may well be outdated. And the sea of professionals clamoring for your business has never been larger.

With over 44 million people in need of some form of mental or emotional care in the United States every year, you would think that there would be enough business to go around. Mental health is big business these days! But since the mid 1980s there has been a 275 percent increase in persons who have trained to provide counseling/psychotherapy.[10] "Turf" wars have grown steadily to determine who will be the top dog in charge of deciding how mental illness will be understood and treated. Unfortunately for the consumer, the confusion over how to best obtain help is slanted toward an agenda that is *secondary* to help. Most of the people who can use help are not able to afford quality care. With soaring costs, people who need help must often choose between eating and medication, or between seeing a human face and taking medications that have side effects. Mental health care has become a problem for the United States, much like its big sister, physical health care. As Barlett and Steel suggest, all of health care has a *Critical Condition.*[11]

Rather than seeking only help and accord for those in need, the mental health profession has become a major industry which mixes profits minded with desire to help. Medication is costly but not as costly as talk therapies might be. So, as a bottom-line issue, biological-pharmaceutical treatments win out, even when it has been proven that the use of both talk and medicine together are more effective. Treatments that focus on strengths leave clients feeling less pathologized, and prevention services can often stop a problem from developing in the first place, but neither are as lucrative for clinicians as a full case load of repeat clients.

In the fight for competitive salaries, and cost containment by third-party payers such as managed care, the dance goes on and on. An hour of psychiatric consultation in the private sector will cost you

Box 3.5
Something You Should Know

Nearly two-thirds of all people with diagnosable mental disorders do not seek treatment. (*Source:* Regier et al., 1993; Surgeon General, 1999)

around $250, while therapy sessions might cost you between $75 and $150, depending on who you see and where you live. We have overdiagnosed, overmedicated, underresearched alternatives, downplayed medications' side effects, elevated the biological-pathological model, and continued the turf wars among the various professions, rather than attempting to be collaborative for the clients' sake.

Gone are many of the components of the ethical codes required by the different professions. Gone are the days when clients had a choice of who they might see. Instead, mental health has become a big business that caters to those with good insurance, or the money to pay for services out of pocket. Left behind are the poor and disenfranchised, and even many in the middle class who could benefit most from mental health services. What we have is a system of nonintegrated ideas, led by groups that have their own financial gain at stake. We have a virtual quagmire of mental health services.

Having said all that, there are, however, many groups of people standing ready to help you, and it is more important than ever to know what they can and cannot do. In the next chapter we look at the different professions, where their roots came from, and what they can do for you.

PART II: TYPES OF SERVICES—PEOPLE, MODES, MODELS, PROCESSES, AND OUTCOMES

Before you make the appointment to see a clinician, you will want to know something about what she or he does, as well as the types of treatment or help he or she can provide. In Chapter 4 we provide a detailed list of all the types of providers, and what they are trained to do, from psychiatrists to substance abuse counselors to hypnotherapists and beyond. When you finish this chapter you will be an expert on the many different fields and clinicians. In Chapter 5 we will discuss the various types of talk therapy, and the real scope on how it works and why. Finally, in Chapter 6 we will walk you through the various types of biological treatments, when and why they should be prescribed, and under what conditions. In this section, we lift the veil of secrecy that sometimes surrounds the mechanics of psychotherapy treatments.

Chapter 4

The Providers

> One simply moves in the direction of accepting one's self more and more completely. Then in the process of this acceptance, sanity simply begins to emerge.
>
> Gerald May (1990, p. 103)

Does the idea of seeing a mental health clinician conjure up ideas of a man in a long white lab coat sitting beside a couch stroking his beard? Or maybe you have visions of Judd Hirsch in the movie *Ordinary People,* gently but firmly telling you that it's not your fault. Clinicians come in all sizes, shapes, colors, and genders, and these dedicated folks see people with all sorts of dilemmas from severe to less problematic. Of course, you want the right one to fit, just like a well-made shoe, so that you will get the best comfort, service, and use, with no blisters to endure.

Several questions typically arise when you look for counseling or therapy. First, who should you go to see? Just who are all the players in this field and who would be best suited for the problem you are dealing with? What sort of treatment do you need? How long will it last? How much will it cost? Do you (or the person you are concerned about) require medication, counseling, psychiatry, or psychotherapy?

If you are a current or return consumer, perhaps the counseling method or approach you tried did not work well or quickly enough for you. How do you proceed from here? The field is complicated, and sometimes one gets specific services based on default situations or because he or she is not an uneducated consumer.

Finding someone to provide services to you is as easy as picking up the phone book. It is filled with names, agencies, and hospitals that are eager to help. But just because someone is listed in the phone book, or they are on a list your managed care company provides you, is no guarantee that she or he will know how to help you with *your* problem or be a good fit for you.

Interesting research may further confound your search. In two meta-research projects comparing the effectiveness of paraprofessionals (psychiatric aides, parents, volunteers, and college students) and professional helpers (psychology, psychiatry, social work, or psychiatric nursing) in the field, both came to the conclusion that there were no significant differences with respect to achievement. In fact, in twelve of the studies analyzed, paraprofessionals faired better. Both studies concluded that trained professionals do not outperform nontrained helpers with respect to their outcome achievement with clients.[1,2] The field of mental health services is full of surprises and interesting twists. However, someone with some clinical training is certainly a good choice, as long as you use your consumer savvy.

In the following section, we will describe how each of the different professionals have been trained, what they can and cannot do for you, where to find more information about them, and potential referral sources. As you have undoubtedly discovered, mental health professionals go by many names. They are trained in different professional fields and use many different techniques. Some of the people in these professional groups have had similar clinical training and use the same techniques as those in other professions. However, there are certain techniques, such as hypnosis, eye movement desensitization and reprocessing (EMDR), biofeedback, and prescribing medications that require extra training or specific education, or can only be executed by specific professions. Knowing who does what and how they view helping you will enhance your consumer skills and leave you less vulnerable to the many competing views in the field of mental health.

The various mental health professionals are listed in alphabetical order. Later in the chapter they will be listed again followed by their respective organizations and Web sites. A description of educational level and courses as well as a brief history and their basic model or belief about therapy is presented.

Mental Health Professionals

Addictions Counselors
Clinical Professional Counselors
Clinical Social Workers
Hypnotists
Marriage and Family Therapists
Pastoral Counselors
Personal Coaches
Rehabilitation Counselors
Psychiatrists
Psychiatric Nurses
Psychoanalysts
Psychologists

All of these professionals are involved in direct clinical service to people needing help, and generically, we call them clinicians.* A lot to choose from, right? Clinicians must go through a process of study and approval at several levels. Lets take a look at that process first.

Two types of governing organizational bodies oversee mental health professionals. These organizations oversee these professions and provide discipline if problems arise, or claims are made against these professionals, such as unethical or dangerous practices, or practices outside the representative organization's requirements. The future clinicians choose to study one of several professions and take a course of study that is in accordance with that profession. Nationally, all of the affiliated professional organizations provide *accreditation,* both to universities and sometimes to the individuals themselves. This accreditation process provides national recognition that the practitioner has graduated from an appropriate and approved school of higher education which meets the standards of the accrediting body. For instance, the American Counseling Association (ACA) has

*According to a report from the U.S. Public Health Service's Center for Mental Health Services, marriage and family therapists comprise 11 percent of the clinically trained mental health personnel in the United States, while counselors and psychologists are at comparable rates (14 percent and 16 percent, respectively). Social workers and psychosocial rehabilitation counselors comprise the highest rates of 22 percent each, while the lowest numbers are shared among psychiatrists (8 percent), and psychiatric nurses (2 percent).

an accrediting branch called the Council for Accreditation of Counseling and Related Educational Programs (CACREP) which accredits universities and graduate programs that provide the education and clinical training appropriate for this discipline. Accreditation guarantees that the person has taken an appropriate course of study as approved by the national organization, at a school that meets certain standards for accreditation.

These bodies may also provide *certification* for individuals. Certification not only recognizes that the person in question has graduated from a school that meets the standards of the organization, and has also done the required field or clinical experience under supervision, but also that they have passed a test that demonstrates a minimum command and understanding of the material that the certification board believes necessary to practice competently.

Now that you understand the process of becoming a clinician in one of the professions, let's look at each of the complementary and sometimes competing professions.

THE PLAYERS

Where possible, we have included information directly from each of the professional organizations' Web sites. Included is information to help you make decisions regarding how the specific profession might be right for you, and under what conditions. But remember, when looking for a mental health professional, you should always feel free to ask questions about someone's qualifications. We will discuss this more in Chapter 9.

ADDICTIONS, SUBSTANCE ABUSE, ALCOHOL AND DRUG COUNSELORS

National Association of Alcohol and Drug Abuse Counselors, (NAADAC)
http://www.naadac.org/

Alcoholics Anonymous
http://www.alcoholics-anonymous.org/

Originating with the Alcoholics Anonymous (AA) movement, addictions counseling is a large and growing profession. There are many addictions counselors who received credit toward their credentials through their own recovery. Within the past two decades, specific training courses for addictions counselors have appeared in universities and community colleges where the specific training can be linked to a degree. Many of the other licensed professionals such as social workers and clinical counselors have taken the specific courses that lead to being certified by their respective state. Licensed psychologists and psychiatrists, and marriage and family therapists have specific language in their licensing codes allowing them to practice in the addictions field. Their training specifically related to addictions may be limited, however, so always ask the key questions outlined in this book.

The history of addictions counseling in the United States (for the nearly 14 million individuals who currently use illicit drugs, the 54 million people aged twelve or older who are binge drinkers, and the 15.9 million people who report being heavy drinkers) begins with the story of Bill W.[3] Bill was an alcoholic who found recovery from his addiction and started the twelve-step group called Alcoholics Anonymous, or AA. After seeking help from some of the best medical people for his "drinking problem," Bill found that what he lacked was a spiritual component in his life. He turned his problem over to his "higher power," devised a program with twelve steps to recovery, and began a society that is now worldwide. AA has been a life-changing program for people of all walks of life that have been unable to stop, control, or limit their use of alcohol or drugs "on their own." Programs for other addicts (all of the following are addictions according to the AA philosophy) include Narcotics Anonymous (NA), Sex Addicts Anonymous (SAA), Gamblers Anonymous (GA), and the vast network of programs for family members, Alanon and Alateen. Addictions are considered to be a primary disease, whereas all other psychiatric or psychological problems that co-exist or are part of a "dual-diagnosis" that are secondary problems. Addiction is also considered a "family disease." It affects the families of addicts—the partners, children, parents and grandparents—in many different ways.

We know that addiction can be understood as having been passed from generation to generation, yet the data regarding treatment models seem to indicate that the treatment of addiction is still an individual endeavor. We will go into this issue in depth in Chapter 5, but you should understand that there are basically four different ideas about how to treat the problem. First, some equate addiction with biologically based therapy. The National Institute for Mental Health (NIMH) has more research programs for biological (medications) treatments than for any other. Second are the "program" people. Usually, these therapists are either in recovery themselves, or have someone in their life that has recovered through the use of AA-type twelve-step programs and continue to follow the steps of AA as a model of treatment. Third are those who choose to treat the whole family. While this group is in the minority, research into the success of a family systems approach to addiction is impressive. Finally are those who advocate "controlled drinking," or Moderation Management as a method or as part of a risk management. In this approach, small steps to reduce the incidence of drinking are considered to be a viable treatment.[4] The debate is strong between those groups who believe that abstinence is the only way–AA programs—and those who see alternative methods as being a useful beginning for a serious and complicated problem.[5] The type of program that an addiction counselor works in will relate to one of the four types discussed previously.

A Word from NAADAC

NAADAC is the premier global organization of addiction focused professionals who enhance the health and recovery of individuals, families, and communities. (NAADAC Vision Statement adopted 1998.)

Addiction is a serious disease and is the number one public health issue in the United States today. According to the U.S. Department of Health and Human Services, Substance Abuse and Mental Health Services Administration (SAMHSA), there were approximately 10.3 million individuals in 1999 with drug or alcohol dependence and 1.6 million admissions to drug and alcohol abuse treatment centers.

NAADAC is the only professional membership organization that serves counselors who specialize in addiction treatment. With nearly 14,000 members and 47 state affiliates representing more than 80,000 addiction counselors, they are the nation's largest network of alcoholism and drug abuse treatment professionals. These experts are working to create healthier families and communities through prevention, intervention, and quality treatment.[6]

CLINICAL PROFESSIONAL COUNSELORS

American Counseling Association
http://www.counseling.org/

Affiliates—American Mental Health Counselors Association
http://www.amhca.org/

American School Counselors Association
http://www.schoolcounselor.org/

Clinical professional counselors are either master's or doctoral-level professionals who have gone through specific education and training to work with clients affected with many types of serious problems.* They may be licensed professional counselors (LPCs), or licensed clinical professional counselors (LCPCs), usually depending on their postgraduate clinical experiences. Professional counselors or professional clinical counselors have taken appropriate course work and a clinical experience under supervision of a senior-level clinician. Most states also require a post-degree clinical experience for at least a year, prior to taking the final licensing exam.

Counseling has roots in education, originating in the vocational guidance movement during the 1800s. During the 1960s, when mental health had a need for more well-trained clinicians, educational organizations that originally prepared school counselors began to develop programs that addressed this issue specifically. These programs are most often accredited by CACREP through the American Counseling Association (ACA). In addition, some programs that were training master's level psychology students were left high and dry when the APA decided to admit only doctoral candidates into the organization as legitimate psychologists. Many programs continued training master's level people, and they were later licensed and/or certified as counselors.

---

*Licensed counselors' training may come from APA-approved master's programs or from an ACA-CACREP-approved program where the degree specialization could be in community, agency, or mental health counseling. Some ACA programs also train family counselors who have the same base curriculum, with additional course work in family counseling. School counselors from CACREP programs also have the basic core classes, but have specialized in working with children in school settings. Professional counselors can be licensed as licensed professional counselors (LCP) or licensed clinical professional counselors (LCPC) depending on the number of supervised postgraduate years in practice.

A Word from the American Counseling Association

What is professional counseling?

Professional counselors work with individuals, families, groups and organizations. Counseling is a collaborative effort between the counselor and client. Professional counselors help clients identify goals and potential solutions to problems which cause emotional turmoil; seek to improve communication and coping skills; strengthen self-esteem; and promote behavior change and optimal mental health. Through counseling you examine the behaviors, thoughts and feelings that are causing difficulties in your life. You learn effective ways to deal with your problems by building upon personal strengths. A professional counselor will encourage your personal growth and development in ways that foster your interest and welfare.

Who are professional counselors?

Licensed professional counselors provide quality mental health and substance abuse care to millions of Americans. Professional counselors have a master's or doctoral degree in counseling or a related field which included an internship and coursework in human behavior and development, effective counseling strategies, ethical practice, and other core knowledge areas.[7]

CLINICAL SOCIAL WORKERS

National Association of Social Workers
http://www.naswdc.org/

Clinical social workers are master's-level professionals. This profession has its origins in working with people who were either destitute or had fallen on hard times because of gaps in social policy. Jane Addams is most likely the most famous of social workers and set up Hull House in Chicago to help those in need. Since the 1950s and early 1960s, social workers have worked closely with the mentally ill in psychiatric hospitals and in community agencies. Their training has a strong emphasis on social policy, group work, and advocacy. They may take a clinical track that trains them for the psychological treatment of people with most types of problems. Social workers have a long history of working within family systems, child advocacy and treatment, and group counseling. Social workers also work in schools doing assessment, therapy, referrals, and linking and planning like those in other areas of social work.

The history of social work is rich and interesting. During the 1500s the beginnings of social work can be seen as church and local governments began to find ways to help the poor and destitute. Elizabethan

Poor Law (1601) gave churches the authority to provide funds and watch over those who were destitute. Charity organizations began to provide assistance through assessment and treatment plans and provided advice and support. This was the first form of social casework. One of the most famous of all social workers was Jane Addams, whose work and activism to help those who were underprivileged was fundamental to the field's growth. As the years passed, social workers' skills with families and groups became important to the field of mental health and social services.

A Word from the National Association of Social Workers

Social workers help people overcome social and health problems, such as poverty, mental illness, child abuse and neglect, emotional instability, illness, economic uncertainty, domestic violence, homelessness, and drug abuse. They work directly with individuals, couples, families, and groups to identify and overcome these problems. Some social workers also work with communities, organizations, and/or systems to improve services and/or administrate social and health programs.

Social workers are found in many settings, including private practice, mental health, schools, community agencies, public welfare agencies, agency administration, and policy and planning. Social work's approach is unique among the helping professions because it focuses on people's problems in the context of their social environment. Social workers believe that people are influenced by the strengths and weaknesses of those around them—their families, communities, workplaces, and organizations.[8]

HYPNOTISTS

The National Guild of Hypnotists, Inc.
http://www.ngh.net/

The National Board of Professional and Ethical Standards
http://www.thenationalboard.com/

American Psychotherapy and Medical Hypnosis Association
http://apmha.com/

Hypnosis is an extraordinary phenomenon that defies a completely satisfactory definition, and debates continue over its nature. Undoubtedly, it can be a useful tool in the hands of a skilled clinician. No one single group claims responsibility or authority over the use of hypnosis, as it should really be considered a technique (Chapter 5), however, some practitioners that use the title of "hypnotist" as a primary category for what they are and do. If you believe you need a hypnotist, you'll want to look for someone that is licensed in one of the other helping professions and who also practices hypnosis. Although licensing is no guarantee of the person's skill level, it does provide you with recourse should you be unhappy with the work.

A Word from American Psychotherapy and Medical Hypnosis Association

Hypnosis is a process during which an individual, usually with the aid of another, allows themselves to become more suggestible. One can experience changes in sensations, perceptions, thoughts, or behavior. Hypnosis is generally established by an induction procedure. Although there are different hypnotic inductions, they are based on imaginative involvement with focused attention and concentration. . . .

American Psychotherapy and Medical Hypnosis Association members provide competent, professional and caring treatment and referrals for treatment, to the clients and patients we serve APMHA offers Certification Training to licensed medical and mental health professionals. It also provides a professional network for licensed professionals to draw on each other's knowledge from different theoretical perspectives and training.[9]

MARRIAGE (COUPLE) AND FAMILY THERAPISTS

American Association for Marriage and Family Therapists (AAMFT) www.aamft.org/

International Association of Marriage and Family Counselors (IAMFC) http://www.iamfc.com/

American Family therapy Academy (AFTA) http://www.afta.org/

There was a time when marriage and family therapy was a technique used by many of the mental health professionals. During the late 1940s and early 1950s a number of practitioners of different professions began to break the mold of seeing individual clients, which maintained the primacy of a private relationship between clinician and client, and opened up the process and people's feelings to one another. Partners actually talked with each other, parents told children what they liked and didn't like about their behavior, and vice versa. And so, systems theory, the notion that the actions of one part of a system affects and constrains other parts of the system, was born as a field of study and treatment.

At first, psychiatrists began to work with the families of clients "with" schizophrenia. Marriage counselors, social workers, and psychologists began to work with whole families, looking into family-of-origin patterns, analyzing how those patterns connected to the present, and then devising all sorts of techniques to help people change. In fact, the emphasis was on change and not on understanding for many of this "new" breed. Instead of understanding psychopathology or problems to be "inside" of people, many began to see the creation of these same phenomena as being constructed within the family, that is, by family-of-origin patterns and the constraints of the nuclear family unit. This notion upset the apple cart of many people involved within the mental health community. Those who saw things as only biological were distressed, those who were family members of seriously troubled psychiatric clients were outraged that they might be "blamed" for their family member's problems, and insurance companies didn't know how to bill for services. Today, of course, most of this has toned down, and family therapists have become a widely accepted profession that has excellent success working with many types of problems. In fact, it is now the treatment of choice for many problems, including adolescent substance abuse, couple- and family-related problems, sexual problems, as well as families of people with schizophrenia. Family therapists were some of the first to use solution focused and narrative therapies, which have become important techniques in the field of mental health treatment. (See Chapters 2 and 3.)

Marriage and family therapists are either master's level or doctoral-level mental health professionals who believe that one of the major ways to help clients improve or change is by involving the family or significant others in the treatment in some form. The family is the context for understanding how or why problems come about, either through unwittingly contributing to the problem by trying to use the same attempted solutions over and over again, even when they have not proved helpful, or by seeing how intergenerational patterns, and recently how groups' repeated stories (myths) about a person or an event can keep a person or group from changing.

Most family therapists maintain a nonblaming stance, analyzing context as a means to assess and change problematic behavior. Marriage and family therapists may have received additional training, or they may have graduated from universities that specifically train both master's level and doctoral-level clinicians.

A Word from the American Association for Marriage and Family Therapy

Marriage and family therapists (MFTs) are mental health professionals trained in psychotherapy and family systems, licensed to diagnose and treat mental and emotional disorders within the context of marriage, couples, and family systems. Marriage and family therapists are a highly experienced group of practitioners, with an average of thirteen years of clinical practice in the field of marriage and family therapy. They evaluate and treat mental and emotional disorders, other health and behavioral problems, and address a wide array of relationship issues within the context of the family system.

Marriage and family therapists broaden the traditional emphasis on the individual to include the nature and role of individuals in primary relationship networks such as marriage and the family. MFTs take a holistic perspective to health care; they are concerned with the overall, long-term well-being of individuals and their families. MFTs have graduate training (a master's or doctorate) in marriage and family therapy and at least two years of clinical experience. Marriage and family therapists are recognized as a "core" mental health profession, along with psychiatry, psychology, social work, and psychiatric nursing.

Studies repeatedly demonstrate the effectiveness of marriage and family therapy in treating the full range of mental and emotional disorders and health problems. Adolescent drug abuse, depression, alcoholism, obesity, and dementia in the elderly—as well as marital distress and conflict—are just some of the conditions marriage and family therapists effectively treat.[10] (Reprinted with permission of The American Association for Marriage and Family Therapy.)

PASTORAL COUNSELORS

American Association of Pastoral Counselors (AAPC)
http://www.aapc.org/

Pastoral counselors are mental health professionals who also are clergy, thus providing a faith-based counseling experience. According to the AAPC, pastoral counseling provides psychologically oriented therapy that includes a religious and spiritual dimension. According to

Gerald DeSobe, PhD, "It is interesting to note that not only is this a time of increased emphasis on therapy, but also a time of increased interest in spirituality. Combining these two areas in a person's life in helpful and healing ways is what pastoral counselors do."[11]

Actually, some of the first mental health "counselors" were clergy, be they mullah, rabbi, priest, or pastor. People generally have gone to their spiritual advisors for answers first. In fact, some cultures prefer to see clergy first, believing that going to a therapist is sharing "dirty laundry" or a sign of weakness.

Clergy are always interested in going to see their parishioners/congregation members when they are ill, and attending to the spiritual part of a person's life as well as the physical or emotional aspects.

A Word from the American Association of Pastoral Counselors

Pastoral counseling is a unique form of psychotherapy which uses spiritual resources as well as psychological understanding for healing and growth. Pastoral counselors are certified mental health professionals who have had in-depth religious and/or theological training.

The American Association of Pastoral Counselors (AAPC) represents and sets professional standards for over 3,000 pastoral counselors and 100 pastoral counseling centers in North America and around the world. AAPC was founded in 1963 as an organization that certifies pastoral counselors, accredits pastoral counseling centers, and approves training programs. It is nonsectarian and respects the spiritual commitments and religious traditions of those who seek assistance.[12]

PERSONAL COACHES

International Coach Federation
http://www.coachfederation.org

Personal coaching is an interesting source of help for some people. With roots in the self-help gurus as well as leadership and business consultants, personal coaching provides people, who can afford the service, a way to get specific motivational help but is not considered therapy or counseling. However, many of the people who provide coaching do have graduate degrees in the mental health field and have begun to practice coaching as a means to help people without the hassle of the managed care or insurance industry. They avoid potential litigation because they call their services "coaching" rather than "counseling" or "therapy."

To those trained in the major fields of mental health clinical work, this service sounds identical to what many licensed professionals do. This is true, especially today, with the current focus on strength-based mental health counseling (see Chapter 7). Coaches are not, however, licensed, nor do they claim to be doing clinical work. Because they do not claim to do clinical work, they don't need to be licensed, hold liability insurance, nor are they required to go through accredited schools of higher learning in programs that have standards adhering to these accrediting bodies.

Coaching professionals meet with their clients in an ever-expanding vista of alternative places such as online, by e-mail, over the phone, through audio- and videotapes, as well as in person. Coaching began as a motivational and goal-oriented service for business professionals, by meeting with them to help them increase their personal goals and financial rewards. Many executives have found the help they need from coaches who help set and attain goals, and stay motivated. With the understanding that most people are not self-starters, have a difficult time staying focused, and tend to lose the edge they need even after serious interventions, coaches provide that kick in the pants to attain business and personal goals—much like an athletic coach who provides a game plan for success for their players.

While clinical therapy has moved on to a shorter-term and quicker intervention strategy indicated by the health care industry, coaching provides the opportunity to engage in expensive longer-term contact without the constraints usually associated with health care.

A Word from the International Coach Federation (ICF)

Coaching is an ongoing partnership designed to help clients produce fulfilling results in their personal and professional lives. Coaches help people improve their performances and enhance the quality of their lives.

Coaches are trained to listen, to observe, and to customize their approach to individual client needs. They seek to elicit solutions and strategies from the client; they believe the client is naturally creative and resourceful. The coach's job is to provide support to enhance the skills, resources, and creativity that the client already has.[13] (Reprinted with permission of the International Coach Federation.)

REHABILITATION COUNSELORS

The National Rehabilitation Counseling Association (NRCA)
http//nrca-net.org/

Commission on Rehabilitation Counselor Certification
http://www.crccertification.com/index.html

Rehabilitation counselors' training includes a master's program in rehabilitation counseling, training in counseling and rehabilitation theories and approaches, and clinical skills to assist individuals with disabilities achieve their maximum level of physical, psychological, social, educational, vocational, and economic functioning. Rehabilitation counselors usually provide individual and group counseling, vocational assessment, case management, and consultation services to persons with any of several types of problems including physical, mental, emotional, developmental, and cognitive disabilities.

Rehabilitation counselors acquire knowledge and skills from several disciplines including counseling, psychology, medicine, education, social work, law, and vocational counseling.

Rehabilitation counselors practice in a variety of public and private settings that include state or federal vocational rehabilitation agencies, private or governmental psychiatric and rehabilitation hospitals, and substance abuse programs. The unique role of a professional rehabilitation counselor promotes self-responsibility and self-advocacy.

A Word from the Commission on Rehabilitation Certification

Rehabilitation counseling is a systematic process which assists persons with physical, mental, developmental, cognitive, and emotional disabilities so that they can achieve their personal, career, and independent living goals in the most integrative setting possible through the application of the counseling process. The counseling process involves communication, goal-setting, and beneficial growth or change through self-advocacy, psychological, social, and behavioral interventions.[14]

PSYCHIATRISTS

American Psychiatric Association (APA)
www.psych.org

Psychiatrists are medical doctors who have earned either a medical doctorate (MD) or a doctor of osteopathic medicine (DO) and are board certified in psychiatry. Psychiatrists can assess, diagnose, make treatment plans, and prescribe medication for psychiatric problems.* Most universities have dropped required course work in counseling or "talk therapy" and have instead moved into treating problems solely on the basis of biological interventions.[15] Psychiatrists can, because of their medical status, hospitalize their clients, even against the clients' will, if the doctor believes it is in the client's best interest.

The term psychiatry is derived from two Greek words that mean, "mind healing."[16] The field of psychiatry began in the late 1700s with an interest in nervous conditions. There were lectures at major universities on human nerves, "moral philosophy of reason," as well as other psychiatric or neurological topics.[17] But the care of those diagnosed with mental disorders was far from scientific or humane, and institutions were really for the purpose of housing and maintaining mentally ill people away from the rest of society, rather than for their treatment. From the beginning, and up until present time, psychiatry has been the study of mental processes that are biological in nature—the brain and its functions. At times, psychiatry and specific psychiatrists have been interested with and influenced by other modes of treatment, but by and large, the field of psychiatry is focused on the biological aspects of the brain, and the means of treatment that is also focused on biology.

A Word from the American Psychiatric Association

A psychiatrist is a physician who specializes in the diagnosis, treatment, and prevention of mental illnesses and substance use disorders. It takes many years of education and training to become a psychiatrist: He or she must graduate from college and then medical school, and go on to complete four years of residency training in the field of psychiatry. (Many psychiatrists undergo additional training so that they can further specialize in such areas as child and adolescent psychiatry, geriatric psychiatry, forensic psychiatry, psychopharmacology, and/or psychoanalysis.) This extensive medical training enables the psychiatrist to understand the body's functions and the complex relationship between emotional illness and other medical illnesses. The psychiatrist is thus the mental health professional and physician best qualified to distinguish between physical and psychological causes of both mental and physical distress.[18]

---

*Psychologists as well as nurses have the right to prescribe psychotropic medication after completing a course on the use and prescription of these medications in some states.

Okay, so now you know what a psychiatrist is, but why would you want to see one, under what condition, and for what reason? Well, let's first look at what the American Psychiatric Association (APA) says.

Another Word from the American Psychiatric Association

Of all the mental health providers in the United States, only psychiatrists are fully licensed medical doctors. Because they are physicians, psychiatrists can order or perform a full range of medical laboratory and psychological tests that provide a complete picture of a client's physical and mental state.[19]*

Harvard University trained psychiatrist Dr. Peter Breggin describes psychiatry this way:

> As physicians, psychiatrists have the right to prescribe drugs or electroshock, to hospitalize clients, and to treat people against their will. They are the only mental health professionals who routinely exercise these powers. Psychiatry sets the tone and direction for the field of mental health and has been rapidly pushing it toward a more biological or medical viewpoint.[20]

According to Breggin, not only has psychiatry continued to push the biological (nature over nurture) part of the field, but it has, at the same time, moved away from "talk therapy." He points out that most universities have stopped teaching anything about psychotherapy, and have moved to the diagnosis and biological treatment of problems with medication, electroshock therapy, and even in extreme cases, the use of brain surgery. Psychiatry is useful in diagnosing and treating severe problems. However, the wholesale belief that all of the major illnesses are diseases, as psychiatrist Nancy Andreasen has proclaimed in her book *The Broken Brain,* is to delimit the notion that psychological or psychiatric problems are overdetermined, a concept so well known in medicine that it can even be applied to the common cold.[21] The medical concept of "over-determination" means that a number of factors—psychological, developmental, biological, emo-

---

*Although the APA Web site states that physicians are the only mental health providers who can prescribe medications, you will also find that in some states trained psychologists as well as some nurses are also licensed to prescribe psychotropic medications.

tional, or environmental—have all come together to produce a problem, rather than there being one final reducible cause.

Many older psychiatrists were taught psychotherapy as part of their arsenal of helping skills, and some of the younger ones have also chosen to learn and practice psychotherapy. Each professional will decide which approach to take and how to work. But to reiterate, most psychiatrists *do not* believe in psychotherapy or counseling as a means to treat problems that are labeled as psychiatric illnesses. So, if you are looking for counseling or psychotherapy—someone to talk about your problems with—you would generally not enlist the aid of a psychiatrist. But again, some psychiatrists are wonderful therapists, so find out first about the people you are going to seek help from, and ask them what they can do for you, and how they choose to practice. Both MD practitioners and ODs or DOs are eligible for psychiatric preparation and training. Advanced residency in psychiatry and passing a qualifying board exam qualifies them to practice psychiatry.

PSYCHOANALYSTS

American Psychoanalytic Association (APsaP)
http://www.apsa.org/

Sigmund Freud, who was wrongly called the "father of psychiatry," launched psychoanalytic theory, which would become known as a the "talking cure."[22] Freud believed that unconscious processes worked out early childhood developmental problems. Freud used clients' dreams, long-term intensive therapy, and an analyst/client relationship, which hopefully unraveled clients' early, mostly sexualized conflicts, to help clients gain insight that supposedly would lead to change. From 1885 to1886, Freud studied with noted hypnotist and neurologist Jean-Martin Charcot, and began to formulate ideas of how the mind works.* In the late 1800s and early 1900s, Freud's work began to take hold, notably with his published *Studies on Hysteria* and his significant progress in mapping out and defining a theory of the mind. Later on Freud published *The Interpretation of Dreams* (1900), and *Psychopathology of Everyday Life* (1901).

---

*Note that a mind is conceptualized as being different from a brain which is a human biological organ of the body.

Today, Freud falls under criticism from most sides, as his highly speculative psychological theories have failed to find support. Of course, he still retains a following: believers in Freud still speckle the intellectual landscape. Yet his impact on society, which was learning a new way of thinking in a modern world, is inestimable. Freud's years of work created a new way of thinking, and challenged the assumptions and suppositions of a changing world. His legacy lives on in the everyday vocabulary and thoughts of millions, despite the drubbing his works have taken.[23]

Freud left us with a number of ideas that have indelibly left their mark on our language, and consciousness, notably the idea of sexual drives, transference, free association, conscious and the unconscious, subconscious, neurosis, ego, super ego, id, sexual repression, suppression, psychosexual development, remaining in therapy until one has completed, and therapy termination. One still hears these words parlayed around in the field, even though the use of psychoanalysis has become somewhat outdated, impractical for most clientele, and unproven as a specific cure for anything.

After Freud came a host of others who were trying to improve on Freud's concepts with their own version of a theory, but the analytic model was by this time deeply imbedded in the consciousness of all that had even a slight understanding of mental health treatment.

Three former colleagues of Freud have left their own legacy, contributing to the ethos of psychoanalytic treatment, and the vernacular with which our culture describes psychological practices. Carl Jung, Alfred Adler, and Roberto Assagioli developed ideas that still are part of the psychotherapy landscape. The major disagreement among these leaders of new analytic movements was usually the emphasis Freudian analysts place on sexuality as a motivator and biological determinant of behavior. Now there are Jungian analysts, Adlerian practitioners, and people who practice the psychosynthesis of Assagioli. Neo-Freudian psychoanalysts, such as Karen Horney, and others, took the classical psychoanalytic ideas of Freud and gave them new life and ideas that are slightly different from what the great doctor Freud intended.

Today, psychoanalytic theory is a fundamental and foundational part of psychotherapy, regardless of the fact that very few people practice it in a pure form anymore. Contrary to popular ideas, few psychiatrists took the analytic road to understand and treat people with what is called mental health problems, but most analysts were, in the beginning, psychiatrists. There are institutions all over the country that teach, graduate, and certify analysts of all kinds, and there are specific short-term trainings that professionals may go through to learn basic skills and theory.

PSYCHIATRIC NURSES

American Psychiatric Nurses Association (APNA)
http://www.apna.org/

Psychiatric nurses have been the backbone of psychiatric hospitalization. They take care of clients by handing out or administering medications, running the day-to-day operations of hospital life, and providing frontline care. The basic educational program for nurses is both scientific and humanistic in content. Most educational programs lead to a bachelor's degree or a BSN—bachelor's degree in the science in nursing. An RN is a designation that the person has at least an associates degree in nursing, and is registered in the state in which he or she practices. Some nurses choose to advance their education to a master's degree (MSN) and even to the level of doctorate, with a PhD in nursing.[24] All educational programs include experience with clients in hospitals, homes, or other settings.[25] As psychiatric care encompassed more than what psychiatrists could provide, psychiatric nurses often facilitated group therapy for clients on the various units, and began to be trained in counseling techniques. Some nurses provide individual, family, and group treatment on an outpatient basis, most often under the direct supervision of a psychiatrist. Although they have been trained to provide counseling or psychotherapy, most have a thorough understanding of mental illness as a biological problem.

Advanced practice registered nurses (APRN) have prescriptive authority to any master's level clinical nurse specialist who has been certified in psychiatric-mental health nursing by the American Nurses Association (ANA) by the majority of states. In some states APRNs are allowed to prescribe and manage psychotropic medications. This may explain, along with the shortage of psychiatrists in some geographic areas, why APRNs are prescribing and managing an increasing share of psychotropic medications in the United States.

PSYCHOLOGISTS

American Psychological Association (APA)
www.apa.org

The common usage of the word "psychological" has been erroneously used to call anyone who provides counseling or psychotherapy a psychologist. But, calling oneself a psychologist requires training from an accredited program in psychology, and then passing a test to gain licensure.

A Word from the American Psychological Association

Definition of "Psychologist"

APA policy on the use of the title "psychologist" is contained in the *General Guidelines for Providers of Psychological Services,* which defines the term "Professional Psychologist" as follows: "Psychologists have a doctoral degree in psychology from an organized, sequential program in a regionally accredited university or professional school." APA is not responsible for the specific title or wording of any particular position opening, but generally, refers to master's-level positions as counselors, specialists, clinicians, and so forth (rather than as "psychologists"). In addition, it is general practice to refer to APA-accredited programs as "APA accredited" rather than "APA approved." The position, as described, must be in conformity with the statute regulating the use of the title psychologist and the practice of psychology in the state in which the job is available.

Definition of "Psychology"

Psychology is the study of the mind and behavior. The discipline embraces all aspects of the human experience—from the functions of the brain to the actions of nations, from child development to care for the aged. In every conceivable setting from scientific research centers to mental health care services, "the understanding of behavior" is the enterprise of psychologists.[26] (Copyright American Psychological Association, used with permission.)

The history of psychology dates back to the seventeenth century when philosopher Thomas Hobbes attempted to establish that for all human phenomena a scientific cause could be found by deductive reasoning. Philosophy giants such as Spinoza and Descartes tied the relationship of the mind to the body. Soon the study of human behavior was completely enveloped by the use of scientific methods and empirical study (observation and testing). Psychological laboratories sprang up at major universities and the new field was legitimized.

In the twentieth century, several ideas pertaining to psychology moved the field along, namely: the behaviorism of John Watson and B.F. Skinner, the Humanist Movement from Carl Rogers, Rollo May, and Abraham Maslow, the social learning theories of Albert Bandura, the rational emotive theories of Albert Ellis, the cognitive-behavioral theories of Beck, and the positive psychology of Martin Seligman and Mihaly Csikszentmihalyi.[27] In addition, the introduction of couples and family work was catching on, and were added to the arsenal of treatments one could choose from. The field of prevention also became a force to be reckoned with, but somehow never became as popular as the one-on-one treatments that dominate the field today. As we shall see later, the work of these psychologists became the basis of many treatment modalities that other professionals used.

Psychologists are a varied group of individuals who work with mental health clients. They must have been trained at the doctoral level. The PhD in psychology (doctor of philosophy) was the main degree that psychologists received, followed later by the EdD (doctor of education). This was grounded in the research and philosophy of the field, until a new APA-accredited program specifically geared to train practitioners began granting the PsyD degree. Psychologists can study *clinical psychology,* which deals with the assessment, diagnosis, and treatment of psychopathology, *counseling psychology,* which has roots embedded in the counseling of persons with less pathological problems, *organizational psychology,* which studies and works with larger social groups, or *social psychology, educational psychology,* and *school psychology.* Although the training is very similar at the core, the emphasis may be different because of the types or groups of people the psychologist chooses to work with. Dr. Martin Seligman's (and others') complaint, resides with the emphasis on pathology rather than on wellness, strengths, or resiliency of individuals. Some psychologists, as well as people from other professions, see a problem with only looking for deficits or problems, rather than looking for peoples' other attributes. Recently, in several states, psychologists have won the right to prescribe psychotropic medication after they have completed a course of study on their use, and prescription.

Psychologists are skilled at testing, also. Psychometric tests can be a helpful assessment to find problems, and therefore provide remediation and therapy.

Like psychiatry, psychology has its critics. Psychology has a grand and full history, and has taken some turns in philosophy that APA's past president Dr. Marty Seligman believes should be corrected. He states:

> In 1947, the National Institute of Mental Health was created, and academic psychologists discovered they could get grants for research on mental illness.
>
> As a result, we have made huge strides in the understanding of and therapy for mental illness. At least 10 disorders, previously intractable, have yielded up their secrets and can now be cured or considerably relieved. Even better, millions of people have had their troubles relieved by psychologists.[28]

Seligman has written several books and articles about the psychological aspects and treatments of mental health problems that have had positive results (outcomes) without the use of medication. His current work is on training clinicians in what he calls *positive psychology,* which asserts that most psychological treatments are based on a medical model that looks for and finds psychopathology and other deficits, when they could be looking for factors that will bring out peoples' resiliencies and strengths.[29]

Pointing out that somewhere along the line psychologists drifted from their previously stated mission, Seligman writes:

> Human beings were seen as passive foci: Stimuli came on and elicited "responses," or external "reinforcements" weakened or strengthened "responses," or conflicts from childhood pushed the human being around. Viewing the human being as essentially passive, psychologists treated mental illness within a theoretical framework of repairing damaged habits, damaged drives, damaged childhoods and damaged brains.[30]

We will take up this point later when we talk about treatments in Chapter 5, but from this chapter's review of psychological thinking, one can see the multiple views of the field, and how people who want and need treatment become confused to the correct path to wholeness.

Why a Quagmire?

Psychiatrists and psychologists have run the general field of mental health since the beginning of modern history. The Surgeon General states:

> Mental illness is a term rooted in history that refers collectively to all of the diagnosable mental disorders. Mental disorders are characterized by abnormalities in cognition, emotion or mood, or the highest integrative aspects of behavior, such as social interactions or planning of future activities. These mental functions are all mediated by the brain. It is, in fact, a core tenet of modern science that behavior and our subjective mental lives reflect the overall workings of the brain. Thus, symptoms related to behavior or our mental lives clearly reflect variations or abnormalities in brain function.[31]

What is troublesome about this is that all of human actions are seen as either abnormal or normal, nothing in between. Because of this, the implication is that all can be treated with biological treatments, or that we can and will at some time in the future, find "cures." This leaves out a great number of competing thoughts about the nature of problems, i.e., cultural differences, family beliefs and teachings, and differing worldviews. Perhaps everything we do, think, or feel *is* a manifestation of how our brains function, but the input of those ideas is not always biological. We are, after all, a composite of how we have learned, what we have learned, and what we wish to believe and maintain as correct and logical.

A question of power and tradition is at stake. The smallest group of stakeholders, i.e., psychiatrists and pharmaceutical companies, make the largest profits from the ever-changing pie of mental health dollars and would try to make out *all* human problems and dilemmas to be biological in nature (see Table 4.1). It is, after all, their training and mission to make the human condition better through the use of biological and chemical means. This method has had great utility and success

TABLE 4.1. Professional Information

Profession	Percent of profession in the field	Approximate Annual Salary	Degree Required
Addictions Counselors	Not available	$36,322**	BA and above
Clinical Professional Counselors	14%*	$43,112**	MA or doctorate
Clinical Social Workers	22%*	$44,268**	MSW
Hypnotists	Not available	Not available	None required
Marriage and Family Therapists	11%*	Not available	MA or doctorate
Pastoral Counselors	Not available	$62,763**	MDiv
Rehabilitation Counselors	22%*	Not available**	MA or doctorate
Psychiatrists	8%*	$148,919**	MD or DO
Psychiatric Nurses	2%*	$79,705**	BSN
Psychoanalysts	Not available	Not available	Doctorate
Psychologists	16%*	$68,165**	PhD, PsyD, EdD

*Data from the U.S. Public Health Service's Center for Mental Health Services.

**The median expected salary for a typical position in the United States as assessed by Salary.com. This basic market pricing report was prepared using survey data collected from thousands of HR departments at employers of all sizes, industries and geographies.

for other physical problems. But, as we will see in the next chapter, there are a number of competing ideas as to the origins of our human problems and dilemmas—with great implications for treatment and even for making a cultural shift in how we understand mental *illness* and mental *health*.

Chapter 5

Talk Therapies: Modes, Models, Processes, and Outcomes

> The mortal wound of psychotherapy occurred when it made objects-to-be-fixed of the people it was trying to help.
>
> Gerald May (1990)

As you will remember from our introduction to this book, there are well over 260 models of counseling/psychotherapy, and most people seeking help have only a vague idea of what to expect.[1] Also, many clinicians, regardless of their profession, may use many of the same methods and common practices. In most therapeutic settings, there will be a relationship between the therapist and client, a shared belief by both parties that something good will come of the experience, rituals such as sitting and talking and perhaps doing some homework in between sessions, and a time expectation for each session. Also, there will be a time line as for how long you will need to be in therapy in days, weeks, or months. Finally, there is commerce—both parties expect to benefit from the relationship. What may be different are the modes used in therapy, e.g., the manner in which it is delivered, and the models of therapy—the different practices based on your clinician's beliefs. The four modes are: individual therapy, group therapy, family therapy, and biological therapy (e.g., medication, surgery, shock treatments), and the models are any of the more than 260 different forms therapy may take (see Box 5.1).

BOX 5.1
Politics of Mental Health

Psychotherapy is a generic term for any approach or technique such as talk therapies or medication that attempts to help people with a bio-psycho-social problem.

QUICK FIXES AND FAST CURES

Regardless of the mode or model, as a consumer, you will want to see some progress. You should experience and expect that you will get help for your money. However, we live in a culture that tends to minimize risks and expects a "quick fix." During World War II a popular phrase declared: "damn the torpedoes, full speed ahead." Somehow our culture has adopted that idea, and it is no more evident than in the field of mental health. We want, demand, and believe we are entitled to fast cures for all our ills with few consequences. If you have a hard day at work, a martini will fix it; get a headache, take a pill; overweight, you can have corrective surgery; feel out of sorts—well you get it! In Western society, we believe that for every problem, a quick and neat cure is appropriate, available, and our entitlement. We are all looking for the silver bullet so that we can get on with our lives.

Many of the therapies available today are "quick fixes" aimed at changing the symptoms that are associated with the problem, but they may not address lifestyle, habitual, or organic issues. There can be side effects and risks associated with quick fixes, but we are conditioned to this way of thinking. It is naive to assume that this mentality is not influenced by "big" health care's desire to profit from our need to have a cure for all our ills.

Most dilemmas that people seek help for are created or maintained by multiple factors. So, consequences also arise from several scenarios. Problems can arise from too little or too much of any of the factors involved. Staying in therapy too long or not long enough can cause problems. Working on only one aspect of your problem when there are multiple factors involved will not provide adequate long-term relief.

Learning Vignette

Sally's husband is a chronic alcoholic who is able to work and provide for the family. Sally grew up in a similar family, where her father was usually drinking and basically unavailable to his family much of the time. Sally, unfortunately, assumed that this was a normal experience. After twelve years of marriage, raising two children with little help, she was depressed and went to see her general practitioner, who, seeing all the classic signs of depression, treated her with medication and the advice to go to Alanon. After taking the medication for awhile (but not the advice), she didn't feel as depressed, but her situation remained the same. The idea of living in this quiet desperation became more and more intolerable, but Sally didn't know what else to do.

Remember, working with only one part of your problem when there are multiple factors involved may not provide adequate long-term relief. Sally could have been helped to understand what a strong and self-sufficient woman she was, or she could have been encouraged to work to get her husband into treatment for his disease, or she could have worked with a clinician to understand and change the way she thought about herself and the family she grew up in, or she could have encouraged all her family to be involved in the therapy, and on and on, all of which would have given her a richer and fuller outcome. Treating one part of the multiple contributing factors can leave you with an incomplete outcome and only short-term relief.

The next potential consequence is how long you need to be in therapy. Again, if you have a longstanding, chronic dilemma you may need to be in therapy using several modes over an extended length of time. Sometimes, however, clinicians will continue to provide you therapy—long-term therapy—when a more direct or useful treatment would work better.

Learning Vignette

Tad was a musician, newly married, and a new father. He had recently lost his mother and grandmother to an auto accident, and was worried that he would never be as good a parent as either of them had been. His father had died when Tad was seven, and he had very few recollections of him. He began having trouble sleeping and sought help for his sleep disturbance. A psychiatrist prescribed a powerful sleep aid, and when that didn't work he suggested that Tad begin talk therapy, referring him to a local clinician.

After two years of counseling, and several attempts at medication changes, Tad was worse off than when he started and now was feeling as if he were a hopeless case. His wife was desperate too. Their sex life was terrible, he could not adequately help out with the household and family tasks, and his marriage was in trouble. He consulted with me on a referral from his pastor, and after a few sessions, I suggested that he consider finding a new cognitively oriented therapist and get a second opinion from a different psychiatrist.

I saw Tad six months later at a local event, and he was doing well. After only three sessions with his new clinician, Tad was feeling optimistic again, and the medication provided by a careful psychiatrist was working. He thanked me for suggesting a change in treatment options and said he believed he might be still seeing the same old two clinicians, and feeling as if *he* was the problem, had he not followed through with my suggestion to seek a second opinion and find a new set of clinicians.

Tad's first clinical team was unwilling to look for alternatives to Tad's problems and continued to treat him with the same tired old treatments. Most likely they blamed Tad for his unwillingness to engage in the therapy *they* chose for him. Like so many clinicians I have known, they assumed that Tad was the problem, rather than considering him to be part of a possible solution.

Not all clinicians see problems and treatments in the same way. Bear in mind that if you are not feeling positive about your care, you should address this with your current clinician and should always feel comfortable in seeking a second opinion. Unfortunately, your insurance company may not provide reimbursement for this or may insist that you see another clinician who is in the same practice group as your current clinician. Even if it means that you spend out-of-pocket money or go to a community clinic where there is a sliding fee scale, peace of mind is worth the price. Not feeling right about the process of therapy will only sabotage your own health.

As you will remember from Chapter 1, problems can be understood from a biological, psychological, or a family/social context. More than likely, it is a combination of these factors that have created or maintained your dilemma. Finding the best method will involve finding the right clinical method, or combination of methods, and that means finding a clinician who will meet your needs. Both you and your clinician will need to make a decision regarding the mode or modes of therapy (will you be seen individually, in a group, or with family participation?), the type of therapy (any one of the currently used, effective models), and how you will participate in the treatment (as a partner in your therapy, or as a partaker).

When you first see a clinician, it is unlikely that you will ask what model or mode of treatment will be used. Most clinicians will make recommendations about your treatment, but most likely you will be eager to move ahead, and may overlook what you are told. Regardless, as you will see in Chapter 7, clinicians are ethically obligated to discuss with you treatment options, risks, and potential consequences of treatment, and obtain your consent to the therapy. So Rule Number 1 for being in therapy is to ask questions about your treatment (see Box 5.2).

Some clinicians may be more *prescriptive* while others are more *collaborative.* The distinctions may depend on your clinician's personality, training, and profession, as well as the diagnosis or assessment of your circumstances. A prescriptive clinician will usually make an assessment or diagnosis of your situation, set up a treatment plan, and then explain it and (hopefully) gain your approval. Like your medical doctor, clinicians will diagnose, plan, and treat according to predetermined protocols. A collaborative clinician will work with you, assuming that your input and involvement are essential to successful treatment. These clinicians may act more like consultants, and will not direct your therapy but will work with you to find the help you need.

If you are comfortable with a clinician who keeps you advised, but prescribes the course of treatment, you will more likely want a prescriptive therapist. If you want to know about your treatment and share your thoughts and ideas about the process, you will be happier with a collaborative clinician (see Box 5.3).

BOX 5.2
Something You Should Know

Feel free to ask questions about the *process* of therapy, such as What form of therapy are you using with me? What are the risks? What sort of success have you had using this method with people who have similar issues to me?

BOX 5.3
Something You Should Know

In business and the world, the bottom line is about successfully engaging clients and satisfying them. Businesses will not succeed if they don't have customer satisfaction. This is not the case in the health care field.

MODES AND MODELS OF THERAPY

Modes: Individual, Group, Family, Medication

There are four common modes in counseling, (including medication). The use of medication will be discussed at the end of this chapter. The three "talking" modes of therapy are individual, group, and family. Most clinicians today have been well trained in individual therapy, though not all have been equally well trained or are skilled at family and group counseling. Clinicians practice what they have been trained to do and because of this, sometimes the most appropriate mode of therapy is overlooked or not used. You will find that some clinicians only use one style, while others will use a combination of styles.

Models of therapy can be seen as frameworks that include a philosophy of what makes people tick and what will help them get better. The models of therapy can be vastly different in the way these components are understood, and we will discuss this a bit more in depth in the next section of this chapter. For now, it is important to know that each of the modes of therapy have models—frameworks—that are usually interchangeable (see Figure 5.1). So, an individual therapist may be using a solution-focused model, while another clinician will provide individual therapy within a psychodynamic framework. Or, a group therapist might be using a narrative framework, while another will use a person-centered model.

Individual Therapy

Most people expect that when they go to see a clinician, they will sit in an office and the clinician will listen to their concerns and help them figure out what to do. This is *individual therapy* and it usually, but not always, comes with the belief that the problem (and the solu-

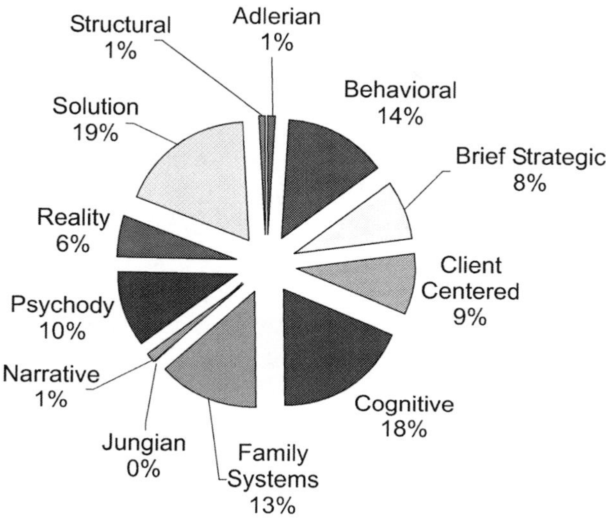

FIGURE 5.1. Models of Psychotherapy Used by Internship Sites Nationally. (*Source:* Edwards, J.K. [2002]. Results of COR Grant. N = 854 National Internship Sites.)

tion) is yours alone, that it resides within you or that you alone will benefit from this one-on-one experience. So, by talking about your issues and gaining insight, or figuring out other ways of thinking or behaving, you will solve your dilemma, change, get better, be cured, or whatever it is that you and your clinician want to happen. Individual therapy is the bedrock of clinical practice, and it is the most commonly used approach.

Group Therapy

Your clinician may also suggest *group therapy,* a mode of treatment in which you will meet with others who are unrelated to you but who may have similar issues. The group will be run or facilitated by a clinician or clinicians, with the idea that you will benefit from talking about your issues and receiving feedback from the group. Groups are also safe places to practice new behaviors. Groups can be highly supportive or confrontational depending on the way the group is run. Groups are very cost effective; you are not expected to pay the same fee that you would if it were individual or family therapy. Groups are also beneficial to the clinician, who may charge each client a reduced or smaller fee than they charge for individual sessions. For example, the individual fee is $100 a clinical hour (a standard fifty minutes). The group rate may be billed at only $50 for each client, but if there are six people in the group, the clinician receives $300. Groups will most often run longer than the standard hour, and sometimes they are offered in what is called a marathon session over a day or sometimes a weekend. The clinician will get billable hourly rates for these. Groups are a powerful means to quick and steady changes that can be enhanced through the use of other modes.[2]

I love being in groups; I love running groups. But I have also seen groups that are very destructive when the leader is not trained, or has an agenda or model that continues to pathologize or scapegoat one or more of the members. Groups can use any of the models of therapy. Be very careful to ask the primary questions outlined in this chapter before starting group therapy.

Family Therapy

Family therapy brings members of the family together to understand and work on problems that involve the family and that will be solved by the family. Family therapy uses a systemic understanding of how problems are created or maintained, as discussed in Chapter 1. Members are brought together in a large group or in smaller configurations, depending on what needs to be discussed. Extended family members, such as grandparents and adult siblings might be seen together, or a nuclear family, a couple, or parents and children, might be the treatment configuration for a time.

Family therapy began as a separate style of therapy, and models grew out of the systemic framework. Over the past two dozen or so years, the models of family work have connected with the general field, melting in and combining with other models. Solution-focused, narrative, brief strategic, and Bowenian models have been used interchangeably in the different modes, so group and individual modes may use any of the models started by family therapists.

Family work is an exciting way of creating and sustaining change. If you understand that a family is affected by, as well as affects the person with the symptoms—the identified patient, as it were—then the concept of working with families is easy to understand.

Learning Vignette

During my early years as a clinician I worked as the primary therapist for a group of emotionally disturbed girls at a residential treatment center. I learned quickly that our team's excellent work and my solid individual therapy could be torn apart as soon as the child was placed back into a home where we had not provided solid family therapy and aftercare.

One of the positive events in the field of family therapy is the shift that occurred over the years toward a framework of collaboration in working with a family's health and strengths rather than always looking for problems that the clinician could "fix." Beginning with the early work of strategic therapists, who believed that a problem could also be seen as an opportunity, the field quickly ran through a number of competing but complementary views. The focus is almost always on what can produce change for people, rather than adherence to a rigid theory.

The field of mental health continues to waffle back and forth on what can really help people. Does working with people's problems and attempting to fix them, or working with people's strengths and helping people maintain them over time work best? Many prominent clinicians from each discipline have become more and more convinced that strengths trump pathology almost all of the time. This framework recently has been used successfully in business, management, education, and health care, and is constantly debated among clinicians in the field.

MODELS, TECHNIQUES, AND FRAMEWORKS

Good grief, there are a lot to choose from! In fact, some clinicians refuse to choose, claiming to be either "eclectic" or "flexible." We touched on what are the most commonly used models in Chapters 1, 2 and 3, and we will not belabor the point. A model, however, provides a framework upon which the clinician begins to understand both the dynamics of your dilemma as well as what she or he believes will help you work toward a better life. A model contains a theory about human nature, how problems arise, and what will help to change, cor-

BOX 5.4
Something You Should Know

A theory is just a model of the universe, or a restricted part of it, and a set of rules that relate quantities in the model to observations that we make. It exists only in our minds and does not have any other reality (whatever that might mean). (*Source:* Hawking, 1996, p. 10)

rect, heal, fix, or relieve you. Your clinician will use one or more of these models to understand you and to help or "treat" you.

Your clinician will also have opinions about other models, and reasons why the model they use is better than others. But, as you will see later on in this chapter, there is not much difference between models when one looks at the final outcomes that each produces.

Several years ago clinical directors from all over the country were surveyed regarding the types of services they offer and the models of therapy they use.[3,4] Figure 5.1 shows how often the most well-known models of psychotherapy are used, as reported by a sample of clinic directors. This type of survey has been administered in different ways over the years, but what remains consistent is that the patterns of use seem to change according to what is "new," what has been researched a great deal, what clinicians are being taught, what managed care companies are willing to pay for, and what is "in vogue." In addition, which models are researched has to do with which are easily researched. Clinicians, it seems, are always looking for more useful and interesting models to use with their clients.

As stated before, there is not much difference between these models in terms of outcome, and there are many similarities. But, there are differences between how much time one is liable to spend in therapy, and what your clinician will want you to do (i.e., focus on feelings, thoughts, behaviors, strengths, or problems). In the end, regardless of mode or model, the process of psychotherapy is helpful; more than 80 percent of psychotherapy clients have significant improvement. However, as we shall see, a great deal of its success is due to the client's efforts.

What are the differences in these models? Differences exist in the way therapists work, understand what caused or contributed to the problem you are presenting, and in the way they should treat you.

Some will see you as having a problem that resides inside yourself, while others will believe that the problem is created by the way people have talked about you, while even others will see the problem as coming from events in your past. Each framework or model will have a different belief about how the problem came about, as well as the best techniques to help. Again, research has shown that there are very few differences in the outcome–how well you do—among different models. In other words, if you were to go to any of the clinicians using the models, you would most likely have the same exact outcome or success rate. Therapy seems to work, no matter what model your clinician uses. In fact, it has been suggested that it is *you, and how you interact* with and chose to work with the model your clinician is using that creates the "magic" of therapy. It is a collaborative effort.

Now, although differences exist, basically, all therapies have the same success with the same types of problems. Rather than go into detail about each model or framework, you, as the client should research some of them, and see which you think would be most helpful to you. A good consumer knows what he or she is buying. Some people we know love Jungian analysis, even thought it is not practiced much anymore, and may not be reimbursed by insurance fully. Others simply want to get it overwith quickly, are highly motivated, and love the positive flavor of solution-focused work. There are enough models to suit anyone, so read up on them. Utilize libraries and Web sites, and find a clinician and model that seem to fit with you. Remember that each framework or model has its believers as well as its detractors. The model has little effect. The relationship you have with your clinician has a big effect. Your willingness to work hard will make a big difference, and part of working hard is to ask questions. Question what your clinician says, have your own opinions, and work with a clinician who makes good sense to you.

THERAPY PROCESSES

Therapy processes are those interesting points that are understood by most clinicians, but are seldom discussed or known by the public. Remember, consumers who are better prepared for their therapy will have even greater success if they understand *all* of the workings and facts. Like magicians Penn and Teller, who lay bare the tricks of magic, once you know how it works, you are more likely to be an active participant.

Psychotherapy and counseling are two words for the same thing. People who say they are providing psychotherapy end up doing the same sort of activities as those who call it counseling. Asking questions, directing the flow of conversation (Did you think you just get to talk, talk, talk?), repeating what you say back to you to make sure you are both on the same page, and perhaps making suggestions or comments are all common components of both.[5] There has never been a study that shows "psychotherapy" is more helpful than "counseling." Some clinicians have been taught or believe that their skills are much better and more "psychotherapeutic" than others, but there is not a shred of evidence to demonstrate that.

During the past forty years, research on the efficacy of psychotherapy has demonstrated its success, with impressive rates indicating that at least 80 percent of patients showed more improvement than a control group (a rigorous scientific condition) who had not participated in therapy.[6] At least 75 percent of the clients improve after twenty-six sessions, while 50 percent show significant improvement after only ten or less sessions.[7] In fact, there is some research that has shown a fair number of people feel better after making the appointment.[8] Hope seems to be a powerful motivator.

People typically remain in therapy anywhere from eight to ten sessions. Many people often go only one time, and it seems that most of those end up feeling positive and get what they want from that one-time consultation. Of course, many clients stay in therapy for a great deal longer (like Woody Allen who all but made a career out of it). But the days of long-term therapy are almost gone for the majority of people. In fact, most clinicians have changed their ideas about having clients stay in therapy for long periods of time. More often today, clinicians have adopted a "general practitioner" or dentist position: clients come in for a time to work on specific issues, and then go out to consolidate their changes. Clients may come back years later when some other dilemma faces them, but by and large the notion that life is full of ups and downs, where professional help may come in handy for a time, is replacing the long-term, "look mom I'm cured" view.

Interestingly, nearly 50 percent of clients drop out of treatment against the advice of their clinician (remember that most of these "drop-outs" felt they got what they needed). There are few predictors of premature drop out, except that people with serious substance abuse or those who are minorities or with a lower education drop out early.[9] Seeking professional clinical help is looked down upon by many cultures, or misunderstood by the uneducated.[10] For some reason, these underrepresented groups don't get the kind of quality, sophisticated care that the upper-middle class may receive. Populations who are in poverty are more susceptible to mental health problems than the general population, leading one to wonder if these conditions are more sociological than medical. We should not underestimate the power of economics and its stresses on people's lives. The economically disadvantaged patient is sometimes treated pejoratively, and does not usually stand up for, demand, or request the services they might need. For example, a single mother, uneducated and on public assistance without many resources will not know what to ask for or how to advocate for herself, while a white, middle-class mother who has a husband and a support system of several generations of extended family members will know how to work the system for herself. I have seen poor, uneducated people who are overjoyed when a clinician finally takes them seriously, and if asked, will tell story after story about how they were ill-treated by past clinicians. And yet there are very simple and useful treatments that can quickly help. Many times, help need not be lengthy, expensive, or complicated.

Your active participation is critical to the process; change is more likely to last if you attribute the ideas of your changes to your own efforts.[11] You are the key to change, more so than anything else that happens, including the clinician you choose or the model used. More influential on a positive outcome than the model of therapy, or even the medication you are prescribed, is your desire to help yourself (motivation), your willingness to engage in the process and believe that help is possible (psychological mindedness), your focus and identification of a problem to work on, as well as the type of dilemma you have.[12] In addition, you will have a better chance of making lasting changes if you have a good social support system, especially a positive, committed relationship.[13]

If you think that a good fit between you and your clinician is important, you would be right, but probably not for the reasons you assume. Although their "bedside manner" is important, what is more important is how *you perceive them*. That's right. If you believe they have your best interest at heart, and you feel that they are really interested in you, you will be more likely to engage in the process. Your *perceived* experience of your clinician's empathy, genuineness, and warmth will add up to the second most important factor for a positive outcome in therapy. Research has shown that the following components are important to the therapeutic alliance: your relationship with your clinician; your capacity to work purposefully during your therapy; your clinician's empathic understanding and involvement; and the agreement on goals and tasks of therapy.[14] You have a wonderful part to play in the positive outcome of your clinical experiences!

The psychological mind-set you have going into your clinical experience also contributes to your potential for a positive outcome. Expectancy of a good experience and even the so-called placebo effect (believing things will improve, even when no real treatment has been provided) will contribute 15 percent toward your successful outcome. Hope is a powerful motivator and controller of your experiences.

The previous saying points to research that demonstrates what you think about something affects its outcome. We are the controllers of our lives; our perceptions control our lives and outcomes.[15] In fact, so powerful are one's beliefs in the possible, that 15 percent of clients experience improvement before the beginning of treatment! Their anticipation pushes them into a better place without ever seeing a clinician.[16]

A huge factor in positive change is believing in your own potential for success, setting realistic goals, trusting the process, and insisting on good care that fits. Any clinician who cannot work with you to get those services and dialogue with you regarding your needs is not worth seeing, in my opinion.

If you think that it is always necessary to see a trained clinician, remember that a significant number of people are helped by friends, family members, teachers, and clergy, all who use a variety of supportive and hope-instilling techniques.

TYPES OF MENTAL HEALTH DELIVERY

You can find help in many different places these days. Types of mental health providers include solo or independent practitioners (this used to be called private practice), integrated delivery systems, community health care or mental health centers, outpatient settings, inpatient settings, and even public schools. Clinicians specialize in almost every configuration of need you could imagine. Clinicians may work in specialty practices for those who have been abused and neglected, sexually abused, are in need of HIV counseling, substance abuse, gay and lesbian issues, family or couples counseling, hospice and grief counseling, domestic violence counseling both for those who are victims and those who perpetrate the violence, youth counseling, weight loss, behavioral health care, and the list goes on and on.[17]

Solo Practitioners

Solo practitioners see clients or patients on their own—sometimes in their own office, sometimes in an office they share with other clinicians in a group practice, and sometimes even out of their home. Solo practice used to be the Holy Grail for clinicians, as it signaled success in the mental health field, and allowed them to practice on their own terms. During the 1970s and 1980s (the golden era), clinical practice rested on a solo practice. Now, as a professor, I need to caution clinicians-in-training about the pitfalls of having a solo practice, and tell them how clinical practice has changed. As other forms of clinical practice came about as a result of insurance changes and managed care "carve-outs," solo practitioners began to struggle for their very existence.

Today, however, many solo practitioners work independently, and provide specialized psychotherapy, which some clients are drawn to, usually without the aid of insurance. For instance, I had a contract with a private substance abuse counseling center, as well as the Department of Children and Family Services, to provide specialized care. These contracts provided me with a nice, steady, extra income from a select group of clientele, very little paperwork, and no hassles for the client or me with the insurance industry.

Other clinicians work within the constraints of some private pay and limited insurance contracts, but the golden days of finding a solo practitioner and an unlimited deal with insurance footing the bill are over. That said, a solo practitioner *can* provide you with services that are simple and easy to obtain. Open any telephone directory and you will find a plethora of clinicians who are more than willing to provide clinical services. With a solo practitioner you will most likely be in a better position to be collaborative in your own care. Use the questions in the last chapter of this book to help you find one that fits your situation and needs. If you need medication, you will need to see a psychiatrist on your own, but if not, solo practitioners are a great source of help. Insurance may pay a solo practitioner, depending on your insurance company and the credentials of your clinician. In some cases, the co-pay may be waived by these clinicians, or your fee reduced, in lieu of going through your insurance coverage. Co-pays are usually high, in relation to what insurance companies are willing to pay for medication-alone therapy.[18] Because of these factors, clinicians are sometimes willing to lower their fees and not get involved with insurance companies at all. As an added benefit, solo practitioners will not have to divulge diagnostic information to your insurance company that might be shared within a massive insurance data system, preventing you from applying for insurance later because of a preexisting condition.

Integrated Delivery System

In an *integrated delivery system,* group practice, or hospital clinical practice, representatives of all the major disciplines are available to you. You will probably be seen first by a psychiatrist (a medical doctor) who will diagnose you and set treatment goals, and make an in-house referral to a social worker, counselor, psychologist, family therapist, or other clinician, depending on the psychiatrist's assessment. If the psychiatrist prescribes medication, you should see that person for follow-up visits on a regular basis to monitor your condition, and assess how the medication and treatment are progressing. You will be charged by the clinic for all services on one bill. An integrated delivery service is the one-stop treatment paradigm of mental health. It is a hierarchy of professionals starting with a psychiatrist, providing services that are integrated to provide more comprehensive care. If you are suicidal, at risk of harming yourself or someone else, psychotic, or out of control, you may be referred or committed to a hospital. Only a psychiatrist can commit you to a hospital against your will, and only if she or he thinks you are at risk for harming yourself, or in serious need of treatment. Depending on the severity of your symptoms, you might be referred to the integrated care group's partial hospitalization program, residential facility, halfway house, or other least-restrictive setting. Here you will continue with your therapy, but your ability to be collaborative with regard to your own treatment will be restricted to a greater degree.

Community Agency

A community agency can and will provide you with services for almost any of the problems affecting you. Many agencies are affiliated with a religious group or larger social service organization. If you are willing to be put on a waiting list, community agencies can provide you with very good psychological help, link you to additional services such as psychiatric assessment and medications, housing, career counseling, etc., and see you for a considerable amount of time, with a sliding fee scale that will fit your needs. Community agencies are an extremely good source of quality care at a reasonable cost.

Termination: A Long-Standing Thorn in the Consumer's Side

An article in *The New York Times* bemoaned how difficult it is to leave a clinician's services—to terminate therapy.[19] Several people in this article discuss their own problems with this phenomenon. My own experiences, both as a client as well as a clinician, confirm what author Susan Saulny reports. For many reasons, for many clients, and for many clinicians, leaving therapy is difficult. Why is this so? Would you have the same sort of reluctance if you were not enjoying a movie or a dinner, or felt you were full or unhappy with what you were partaking? Would you sit it out and wait till it was over or until someone else told you it was alright to leave? What if you knew that the next week and the next week and the next, you had to pay for and endure the same sometimes painful event again, with no end in sight?

There was a time, and this is the core of the problem, when termination came at the end of a long, several-days-a-week analysis, and signaled that you were "done." As therapy models have evolved and managed care has insisted on fewer sessions, the premise of endings is not a clear one. For clinicians, private practitioners especially, endings mean two things: (1) a lull in the paycheck, and (2) searching for or accepting a new patient to fill your place. But as a consumer, therapy is about you, not your clinician. You have the right, and in fact the responsibility to say when enough is enough.

To give the devil his due, if you are unhappy with your services, you should, at the very least, ask for a session to discuss your qualms, and perhaps even have a friend present. Several clinician friends have given a client a free session to assess the therapy. Talking about the possibility of leaving therapy needn't be a long, drawn-out event, just several minutes to address your concerns, why you are thinking about leaving, why you are not satisfied, etc, and a rebuttal time without guilt trips from your clinician. If your clinician is aboveboard, and strives to be up front and collaborative, you will be less likely to have this sort of problem. In fact both the clinician and you should keep in mind the goals that you are both working toward, when you will know if you are getting close to going it alone, or more likely, when your insurance is reaching its limit, (and what you should do when it does). Remember: therapy is a business for your clinician. This is the way he or she earns a livelihood.

Another reason for termination could also be that you have come to a "turning point" and the clinician does not have the clinical experience or training to take you further. This sort of thing happens sometimes, and a good referral to the next type of services can build upon the work you have done with your first clinician. Individual therapy can turn into group work, or into specialty services such as family therapy, substance abuse work, or working through past traumas. In this type of termination, you should feel successful to have come to such a place where you are able to move on to new understandings of your process and changes.

Termination of your therapy work should be a happy occasion or a turning point. Some serious reasons for leaving your therapy, aside of your successful completion, are inappropriate behavior by your clinician, working in a clinical direction other than what you have contracted for, not getting good and timely feedback on your progress, and therapy going on and on without any improvement. No improvement after a few months should be a signal that something is not working. Over half of all clients find they are improving within ten sessions, and three-quarters find they have improved significantly after a little over six months. If you are not experiencing some success, you need to move on, find a new clinician, and set some new, more achievable goals.

Inappropriate conduct from clinicians can come in several forms, and range from not listening to your concerns, talking about their own issues more than they talk about yours, all the way up to the most inappropriate of all, sexual harassment or inappropriate sexual advances. Sexually inappropriate behavior does occur, even though it is an ethical violation for every single professional in the field. This will be covered in Chapter 7.

If any of these occur during your therapy, you should stop the sessions immediately. If inappropriate sexual contact or advances have been made, report the clinician to your state mental health board of professional regulations, as well as your clinician's national and state organization.

This ends the discussion of the talk therapy treatment process. Next, we will discuss the use of medications, and its pros and cons.

Chapter 6

Biological Treatments

> Violence, for example, is not considered a "mental disorder," but I expect that more lives are ruined annually by it in the United States than by depression. And why aren't bad marriages, cowardice, explosive anger, dishonesty, lack of work ethic, and the like the focus of more federal prevention efforts?
>
> Martin E. P. Seligman (2001)

Before we tackle a discussion on the use of medication, let us make a few disclaimers, as well as some observations. This author (Jeff) has been in the mental health field for over thirty-eight years. I have worked at and directed agencies including residential treatment centers and day-treatment programs for children and adolescents and their families in which medication was not used at all and behavioral and relationship treatments were the only methods used. Talk therapy works very well most of the time, and yet medication has become the method du jour. Medications do what they are supposed to do quickly, most of the time, but almost always with some form of consequence. However there is a lot of "deep-pocket influence" in the use of medication (see Box 6.1). Client choice is, more often than not, swayed by the current culture, rather than based on consumer research of options. As previously discussed, problems can be attributed to three sources (see Chapter 1, 2, and 3). The established model today is a bio-psycho-social model, which has been around since World War II, when the treatment of shell-shocked soldiers demonstrated that emotional stresses could present as a physical condition. Later, in 1977, George Engel published a well-received article in *Science* asserting that there are multiple determinants in the development of diseases.[1]

BOX 6.1
The Politics of Mental Health

We object to marketing and corporate influence holding sway over public and professional opinion when the data regarding both the theoretical underpinnings and efficacy of drug treatment is at best unconvincing. Further, we fully recognize that medication helps some clients and that they freely chose drugs as a first line of defense. In truth, we honor client preferences, even for medication, and stand against any practice that does not center clients' desires about how thy may be helped. (*Source:* Duncan, Miller, & Sparks, 2004, p. 147)

Although we may indeed know that problems come from several converging sources, the field has been taken over by those who want biology to be seen as the primary cause of human suffering, or at least for the first line of treatment.

For instance, medications for depression are prescribed *in excess* of actual need.[2] General primary care physicians (PCPs) prescribe more psychotropic medications today than psychiatrists, spend less time with patients (twelve to fifteen minutes), and have difficulty in recognizing or managing serious mental health concerns of their patients. Add to this the fact that almost half of all patients treated with current antidepressant medications report having side effects and that more than half skip doses or stop taking their medications as prescribed.[3] When one views this with the affirmation that, at present, fourteen major "mental illnesses" can be effectively treated with psychotherapy, or improve outcome potential when combined with medication, our problem as a field becomes apparent.[4] In addition, prevention strategies are highly effective for several psychological problems, alleviating the need for primary "treatment" completely.[5] And yet the use of psychotherapy has declined, even when there is evidence that psychotherapy increases the effectiveness outcome.[6] The reasons are clear. Patients no longer have much of an option, as insurance usually requires high co-pays for psychotherapy, but not for medications.[7]

PROBLEMS WITH A BIOLOGICAL MODEL

Our culture is in a quick-fix mode and focuses on problems or pathology. The turf wars over which view will be in charge are evident in how research money is used by the National Institute of Mental Health (NIMH). In 1990 the previous administration, which was directed by a public health physician, was replaced with a new, more "biologically oriented" administration. In fact, the new director of NIMH dubbed the 1990s the "decade of the brain," indicating that all research endeavors were now to be directed toward brain chemistry and biological problems that "caused" mental illness.[8] The NIMH researchers were looking for cures, of course, stating that it is chemistry, not environment or other factors that matter most. Instead of looking at relationships or the learning of the mind, they searched biology, defaulting to chemistry and symptoms, and more recently to genes. In essence, even though there is a genuine interest in being helpful, there is also a vested interest in maintaining the hierarchy of deep-pocketed biological-model interest groups that is the current version of our mental health system (see Box 6.2).

Most psychiatric conditions do not have a clear etiology; rather, they are defined as either syndromes or patterns of symptoms that include emotion, cognition, perception, and/or behaviors.[9] As the American Psychiatric Association's *Diagnostic and Statistical Manual of Mental Disorders* (DSM) states: "The problem raised by the term 'mental' disorders has been much clearer than its solution, and, unfortunately, the term persists in the title of DSM-IV because we have not found an appropriate substitute."[10] In addition, it states, "In DSM-IV, there is no assumption that each category of mental disorders is a completely discrete entity with absolute boundaries dividing it from other mental disorders or from no mental disorder. There is

BOX 6.2
Politics of Mental Health

Despite fifty years of research, the invention of electron microscopy, the advent of radiolabeling techniques, the revolution of molecular biology, and the merger of computers with neuroimaging machines, *no* reliable biological marker has ever emerged as the definitive cause of any psychiatric "disease." What many fail to appreciate is the biochemical imbalances and other so-called functional mind diseases remain the only territory in medicine where diagnoses are permitted without a single confirmatory test of underlying pathology. (*Source:* Duncan, Miller & Sparks, 2004, p. 167) also no assumption that all individuals described as having the same mental disorder are alike in all important ways."[11]

The main biological treatment model available is medication, a physician-determined treatment, except in those states where psychologists have won the right to prescribe medication when they have had additional training.

The use of medication has been a boon to the field of psychiatry and biological/behavioral/mental health in treating a wide variety of symptoms of major disorders. Medication provides a relatively quick and easily accepted treatment for many dilemmas of the psyche, all with limited contact of a human relationship, without the sharing, self-disclosure, and caring as a part of the treatment. However, with medication are always a possibility of side effects such as sleep disturbances, sexual dysfunction, dry-mouth syndrome, and more.*

So why do we believe medication is useful, safe, and the treatment of choice? First, all medication, like food, is checked by the United States Food and Drug Administration (FDA), which is also a part of the United States Department of Health and Human Services, of which the National Institute of Mental Health is also a part. All medications are subjected to at least two independent (not conducted by the manufacturer) clinical trials to ensure their effectiveness and safety.

The research for and against medication is varied, and generally written from points of view—really opinions—rather than from any straightforward, easy-to-make-sense-of facts. Two camps, those on the biological side and those on the talk-therapy side, have research showing effectiveness of their "product" as well as reasons why their point of view is most trustworthy. They also demonstrate why the other side's point of view is not.

One side—the biological side—points to clinical trial research to show the effectiveness of medications. Academic researchers provide clinical trials demonstrating the effectiveness of the medication under question. Medications are approved by the FDA when two or more clinical trials show positive results. Because clinical trials require testing on live patients, research is usually conducted at university medical clinics. Researchers in these facilities are faculty members who are required to get grant funding and to publish these

*When taking any medication, it is advisable to carefully read the enclosed brochure for possible side effects, and log on to the company's Web site. If you have questions, refer to your physician for specific answers, and always report any side effects you have.

BOX 6.3
Politics of Mental Health

In the past fifteen years, HMOs, insurers, pharmaceutical companies, hospital corporations, physicians, and other segments of the industry contributed $479 million to political campaigns – more than the energy industry ($315 million), commercial banks ($133 million), and big tobacco ($52 million). More telling is how much the health care industry spends on lobbying. It invests more than any other industry except one, according to the nonpartisan Center for Responsive Politics. From 1997 to 2000, the most recent year for which complete data is available, the industry spent $734 million lobbying Congress and the executive branch. (*Source*: Barlett & Steele, 2004, p. 69)

findings, so they are under considerable pressure to keep their jobs. Research is almost always funded by the manufacturers of the medication. However, the researchers are held to strict scientific standards with a requirement to disclose the source of their funding. This is standard procedure, and the government as well as the researchers have attempted to find a way to not only get fair clinical trials, but also to demonstrate that what they are doing is aboveboard, even if their funding is from the manufacturer of the drug they are testing. Because a dual relationship might influence the researchers to show evidence in favor of the medication, publications must list the source of the research funds.

On the other side, those who advocate against the use of medication are clearly in favor of talk therapy over medication. One group of writers points to a number of problems that are associated with research on drugs.[12] These problems include, first, that most of the ratings of improvement during medication trials are clinician ratings rather than client/patient ratings. Studies have shown that clinicians and clients can differ a great deal in their evaluation of improvement and effects. Second, compromised research conditions, such as a blind trial in which both clinician and client are not supposed to know if they are getting the real medication or a placebo, may not be so blind. According to several studies, the clinical blind is not so blind, therefore invalidating the scientific objectivity of the research. Third, the length of time of clinical trials is different than that of actual use, calling for longitudinal research for better control and more accurate results. Fourth, conflict of interest as we have discussed, is widespread, in that those who study the medications may feel pressure to show significant positive treatment results because their funding source is the manufacturer of the medication who, of course, wants a favorable result.[13]

In addition, if you take a look at any of the medications used for depression, for example, you will see how the drug companies, in order to comply with FDA standards, may not specify that the problem they aim to treat is "caused" by a biological problem. Instead, they state several vague and leading statements such as: "Depression and anxiety disorders might be caused by a chemical imbalance in the brain"; or "The exact cause of these conditions is not completely understood. Research has shown that depression and panic disorders could be linked to a chemical imbalance in the brain. A family history of these conditions might also play a role in their development" (we hope you notice the words "might" and "could be" in the above added for emphasis).[14] If you do an Internet search of any of the leading manufacturers of medications used for mental illnesses, you will find similar statements, as truth in advertising prevents them from making definitive statements about the cause. The DSM specifies that it is multicausal, with the possibility of several combined etiologies (roots).

In medicine, the study of pathology is organized by organ systems. Yet behavioral health researchers and practitioners code/term using syndromes or symptoms because there is no definitive body part to point to. Even though there are multiple treatments to attend to the multiple causes, the trend is toward the use of medication, even though there are alternatives. It has been our experience as well as our perception that people, and the mental health profession, are firmly embedded in one of three camps. First are those who move quickly to acceptance of medication or whatever a health care professional (usually a physician) suggests. This is the quick-fix group who believe that medicine and the physicians who prescribe them are the most helpful, safest, and best treatment available. These folks trust and respect the physician implicitly. The second group is the complete opposite of the first group; people in this group believe that the use of any medication is dangerous, if not poisonous. These people will suffer any pain while they attempt to find a safe alternative. They do not want to ingest any foreign substance into their body. They avoid medications and watch what they eat. The third group is somewhere in the middle, having a guarded optimism about their life and surroundings, checking out for themselves the information about their own treatment, weighing the consequences and potential usefulness of all treatments, and carefully discussing the options with several mental health professionals. These people take responsibility for their own treatment choices and operate from an informed perspective. We wish that more people were like this (see Box 6.4).

MEDICATIONS: PROS AND CONS

The use of medication is currently *the* most flourishing treatment, and, as a consumer you should be well informed. If you are currently taking or are considering medication you should know what the medication is, what its supposed to do, the dosage, how it should be taken, common foods or supplements you should *not* take with it, as well as potential side effects and risks. Medication has changed the lives of many patients. Medication may help make counseling more effective, or it may improve symptoms so the patient can relate with others better. Although, medication *does not cure* mental illness, it can reduce symptoms, get rid of "voices," make the world seem clearer, reduce anxiety, or lift heavy depression. The degree of response, ranging from a little relief to complete relief, as well as how long someone should be on medication, depends on the individual and the type of problem being treated. Some medications may relieve symptoms right away, while

BOX 6.4
A Teaching Vignette

Jay was a psychologist who had bipolar episodes he concealed from everyone. When I first met Jay, I thought that something was strange about him, as he always smelled like incense and was usually a *very* upbeat kind of guy. But there were also times when he seemed sad and removed.

Finally it happened. Jay was found running around a community park naked on a balmy rainy evening. He then came clean with the facts that he had large mood swings and had used alcohol and marijuana in various combinations in an attempt to medicate himself. It wasn't working, and Jay was arrested, embarrassed, and almost lost his job.

others may take as long as six weeks to begin helping. Sometimes a second medication may be prescribed to counteract the side effects of the primary medication. For many depressed or anxious patients, medication may be needed for several months and then never needed again, or it may be needed for longer periods of time. Patients who have more serious problems may have to take medication for the rest of their lives, as well as continue with supportive talk therapy. All medications and combinations of medications should be monitored at all times by the prescribing health care professional.

Medications are prescribed for four large categories of problems: (1) antianxiety medications, (2) antidepressant medications, (3) antimanic medications, and (4) antipsychotic medications. Again, medication does not "cure" the problem, it alleviates the symptoms by either removing them, making them less pronounced, or by shortening the length an episode occurs. In this discussion, we will use the brand names rather than scientific names, as that will probably be most familiar to you as a consumer. Also, be aware that new medications are always becoming available, sometimes there are name changes of medications, and your health care professional may also use a medication "off label," that is, using a medication for the treatment of a problem for which it was not intended.

You should always discuss your medicine with your prescribing clinician, ask for potential side effects, what the medication does and how it works, how long you will be taking it, what foods you should avoid, and how alcohol or other drugs affect the medication. Medications are powerful treatments, and they can be potentially dangerous or addictive in some cases. Be informed and treat them with respect. Do not, under any circumstances treat yourself by using someone else's prescription, your own concoctions, alcohol, or street drugs, or take yourself off medication without consulting your health care clinician.

A complete list of psychiatric medications, their common and chemical names, and how they work can be found in the *Physician's Desk Reference* (PDR) at any public library and at the National Institute of Mental Health Web site.[15] You should not only read and learn about the medication and treatment you might use, but read and learn about several alternatives, discuss your options and treatment possibilities, and the benefits and risks with *all* of the mental health clinicians you see.

It is generally believed that medication works by changing the chemical composition in the brain. These chemicals, called neurotransmitters act like messengers between nerve cells. They are metabolized in the brain, and may be a factor in some emotional and mental problems. Medications alter the processes of these neurotransmitters so that the brain might use them, store them, or release them more efficiently. It is thought that altering these processes relieves symptoms.[16]

When using medication, always be aware of the potential for side effects and, if you experience any, report them immediately to your prescribing health care professional. Never discontinue medication until you have discussed this option with your prescribing clinician. Any other medication, including over-the-counter vitamins, should also be reported to your clinicians.

FREQUENTLY PRESCRIBED MEDICATIONS

Following are the four major behavioral problem categories, the DSM-IV-R code used for each, the types of medications frequently prescribed, as well as how they work and potential side effects.

1. *Anxiety Disorders* (with DSM-IV-R codes). *Panic Disorders* [300.01], *Obsessive-Compulsive Disorders* [300.3], *Post-Traumatic Stress Disorders* [309.81], *Social Phobias* [300.23], *Specific Phobias* [300.29], and *Generalized Anxiety Disorders* [300.02] affect approximately 19 million American adults.[17]

Antianxiety Medications

Both antidepressant and antianxiety medications are prescribed in the biological treatment of Anxiety Disorders. Obsessive-Compulsive Disorder may be treated with the tricyclic antidepressant Anafranil, or the SSRIs, Prozac, Luvox, Paxil, and Zoloft. Anti-depressants, such as Paxil, are also used to treat Social Phobia, General Anxiety, and Panic Disorders, while Effexor, which affects both norepinephrine and serotonin can also be used for General Anxiety.

Benzodiazepines such as Klonopin, Xanax, Valium, and Ativan are commonly used in the treatment of anxiety either as a daily regimen or "as-needed," where they enhance the activity of the neurotransmitter GABA.

Possible side effects of benzodiazepines include hypotension, numbness, drowsiness, weight gain, apathy, dry mouth, and sexual dysfunction. *When taking these medications, do not drink alcohol, as the two can become a lethal combination.* Benzodiazepines can lead to dependency, and withdrawal reactions can be very difficult. Do not stop taking these medications on your own, and always discontinue use in conjunction with your prescribing clinician's help. If you have any symptoms of side effects consult with your prescribing clinician immediately.

The latest medication in the current treatments of anxiety, BuSpar, is neither an ant-depressant nor a benzodiazepine, and is used in a regimen that needs several weeks to become regulated and consistent.

Antidepressant Medications

2. *Depressive Disorders* (with DSM-IV-R codes). *Major Depression* [296.xx] or Dysthymia [300.4] affect 18.8 million American adults, or 9.5 percent of the United States population.[5]

Major depression is the sort of problem that most likely benefits from treatment with medication, though milder forms of depression may be treated with medication as well. Antidepressants reduce symptoms so that people are not quite as debilitated. Usually these medications begin to take effect after a few weeks, but only reach their full effectiveness after six to eight weeks. Again, as with other medications, it is important to follow the prescribing health care professional's instructions, not skip doses, or discontinue treatment without his or her help.

Early on, tricyclic medications such as imipramine, amitriptyline, nortriptyline, and desipramine were used to affect two neurotransmitters, norepinephrine and serotonin. Tricyclics are effective in treating depression, but they have some fairly unpleasant side effects. Other medications known as monoamine oxidase inhibitors (MAOIs) such as Nardil, Parnate, and Marplan have far fewer side effects, and are effective for major depression when other medications have not worked, however the potential side effects of MAOIs make its prescription limited to a small number of patients. When using MAOIs, it is important to check to see which foods and beverages are safe to eat, as serious problems can occur.

Recently, several newer antidepressants with fewer side effects, called selective serotonin reuptake inhibitors (SSRIs), such as Prozac, Zoloft, Luvox, Paxil, and Celexa, have become the treatment of first choice. These medications affect the serotonin level in your brain. Most recently, a new set of medications, like the earlier tricyclics affect norepinephrine and serotonin, but with fewer side effects. Effexor and Serzone are less likely to produce a host of side effects, but Serzone, can cause liver failure, which can be life threatening. Medications like, Remeron, a sedative, and Wellbutrin, are now a safer alternative for some patients if they have not had seizures in the past.

Tofranil, Anafranil, and Elavil inhibit the uptake of norepinephrine and serotonin at the synapse in the brain, and possible side effects include dry mouth, constipation, urinary problems, blurred vision, and nasal congestion. Prozac, Zoloft, and Paxil inhibit the uptake of serotonin in the brain and can have similar side effects, such as dry mouth, constipation, and urinary problems, but they are less common and less severe. Nardil and Parnate increase neuropinephrine and possible side effects include hypotension, dizziness, dry mouth, upset stomach, weight gain, blurred vision, and headaches. Foods such as cheese, beer, wine, some vegetables, packaged soups, sour cream, and yogurt can be a fatal combination when ingested with this last set of medications.

The drive for a perfect medication is on, but probably is not going to happen. Each person is different, and the side effects or lack of them are cunning, ever present, and require open communication and feedback with your prescribing health care professional. It is important to read the information enclosed with your medication, discuss the potential for side effects, and have a plan of what to do in case you have an adverse effect, and follow the treatment regimen specifically. Finally, know what sort of foods and beverages you should not take with any medications you are on.

Antimanic Medications

3. *Bipolar Disorders-Manic Phases* (with DSM-IV-R codes). *Single Manic Episode* [296.0x], *Most Recent Episode Hypomanic* [296.40], *Most Recent Episode manic* [296.4x], *Most Recent Episode Mixed* [296.6].

Typically, antimanic medications are used to treat bipolar disorders. People who have this sort of problem have mood swings from very high manic moods to very low depressive moods. Usually, people may stay in one of these two moods for long periods of time, or may cycle rapidly, back and forth. Lithium has been the medication used most often to even out the mood swings. Lithium can reduce severe manic symptoms in five to fourteen days, but may take weeks or even months before there is full relief. Sometimes an antipsychotic medication is used at first to help gain control of the manic symptoms until the lithium takes effect. Also, antidepressants can be used with lithium to help the depressive mood cycle of this disorder. It is extremely important that regular blood tests are done when using lithium.

Possible side effects of lithium include drowsiness, weakness, nausea, fatigue, hand tremor, and weight gain. Kidney changes may occur, increased urination, and lithium may affect the thyroid gland. Increases in the consumption of table salt or the use of diuretics can increase the lithium level, causing some severe problems, including the potential for death.

Occasionally, people with manic symptoms who cannot or do not want to use lithium respond to anticonvulsant medications used for seizures, such as Depakote. Although Depakote is effective, it too has side effects that need to be watched. Tegretol, Lamictal, Neurontin, and Topamax are anticonvulsants that work best with acute manic symptoms rather than for long-term maintenance.

Your clinician may also prescribe other medications, along with mood stabilizers, for anxiety, depression, or other problems. As with other medications, it is important to stay on the treatment unless discussed with and agreed to by your prescribing clinician. Very serious problems can occur with the thyroid and liver, requiring the patient to have continued medical monitoring.

Antipsychotic Medications

4. *Schizophrenia and Other Psychotic Disorders* (with DSM-IV-R codes). *Schizophrenia* [295.xx], *Schizophrenia, Paranoid Type* [295.30], *Schizophrenia, Disorganized Type* [295.10], *Schizophrenia, Catatonic Type* [295.20], *Schizophreniform Disorder* [295.40], *Schizoaffective*

Disorder [295.70], *Delusional Disorder* [297.1], *Brief Psychotic Disorder* [298.8].

A number of antipsychotic medications are available. These medications affect neurotransmitters in the brain, which allow nerve cells to communicate with one another. One of these neurotransmitters, dopamine, is thought to be relevant to schizophrenic symptoms. The medications Thorazine, Mellaril, and Haldol can have serious side effects, such as tardive dyskinesia, which is a permanent involuntary neurological movement disorder, affecting walking and facial movements. Because they have fewer side effects, new medications, called atypical antipsychotics have become available and are often used as a treatment of choice. Clozaril is usually more effective for individuals who do not respond to other medications. However, people who use Clozaril risk a serious blood-disorder side effect, and therefore must have a blood test every one or two weeks.

Several other atypical antipsychotic medications such as Risperdal, Zyprexa, Seroquel, and Geodon are now on the market, each with its own potential side effect risks. Some may be tolerated better than other medications. These drugs do a good job in treating symptoms and side effects are most often mild. According to most researchers, the side effects usually become less pronounced, and may even disappear after a few weeks.

Medication for Children and Adolescents

The biggest debate around the use of medication most certainly pertains to the medicating of children and adolescents. A few, common psychiatric problems are seen in children; we will discuss them briefly. Although there is disagreement among professionals regarding medicating children, there is not a disagreement that a team of mental health professionals is essential to their treatment. The treatments may include medications and psychotherapy, parental consultations, family group therapy, all based on the child's and family's needs. Because of the risks involved in taking medications, it is extremely important that all members of the team, including parents, guardians, teachers, and other clinicians stay alert for signs of side effects. Children and even adolescents may not discuss the problems they are having readily, and for that reason, good communication and vigilance are important for all involved.

Several things should be considered before making the decision to use medication when confronted with a child's disruptive, depressed, or odd behavior. According to the NIMH, scientists have discovered developmental changes during late adolescence which include a second overproduction of the brain matter that has to do with thinking, as well as planning, impulse control and reasoning.[18]

The many changes during this period of childhood and adolescence are important. Serious executive functions needed for a satisfactory life are developing at this time. The effects of medications on the emerging growth and development of the brain in children and adolescents are unknown.

Next, gauge your child's behavior against other children you know, and ask teachers, friends, and health care professionals if the behavior is very different from other children's. Childhood, and especially adolescence, is a difficult time during which most of our learning about the world occurs. Does the use of medication teach youngsters that human problems need to be dealt with a pill, or can they learn from their situations about problem solving?

Finally, is the problem really serious to the point where something has to be done? Many parents are reluctant to seek help. If my child were showing signs that he or she was depressed, or talking about suicide, I would move mountains to get the help he or she needed. However, the effectiveness of medication may take time, and even though it can be, overall, a helpful therapeutic, do not overestimate it. The lag time between the first dosage and when the medication begins to do its work may require that other avenues be taken. No one likes to start out a child's life with a diagnostic label, which can undermine a child's confidence and provide a diagnostic stigma for teachers and relatives to use. But, not deciding to act is also a decision. Make any decision with relative speed and with tons of input. Be informed, make your decisions, and be involved.

Childhood depression and anxiety are increasingly recognized and treated. However, the most common problem treated among children is attention-deficit hyperactivity disorder (ADHD). Medications most often prescribed for ADHD are stimulants, which have a reverse effect with children. These drugs can settle them down and help them focus. The common medications for this problem include Ritalin, Metadate, Concerta, Adderall, Dexedrine, Dextrostat, and Cylert. Cylert has the serious potential side effect of liver damage. Antidepressants such as Wellbutrin may be used instead of stimulants for those children who are not responding well to other courses of treatment. Strattera is a nonstimulant medication. It is a selective norepinephrine reuptake inhibitor that strengthens the chemical signal between nerves that use norepinephrine to send messages.

Attention-deficit hyperactive disorder is, according to many professionals, the most overdiagnosed childhood problem.[19] Although the NIMH continues to do MRI research on adolescent brains, it still maintains that medication is a useful treatment.[20]

The debate over the prescribing of antidepressants for children is still raging. Those in favor and those against hold their views. Some favor what the clinician believes to be true, and cite research that can bolster their arguments. At the same time, the NIMH has cited the FDA's warning about the potential of suicide when using medication with adolescents, stating:

> Recently, concerns have been raised that the use of anti-depressant medications themselves may induce suicidal behavior in youths. In fact, following a thorough and comprehensive review of all the available published and unpublished controlled clinical trials of anti-depressants in children and adolescents, the FDA has warned the public about an increased risk of suicidal thoughts or behavior in children and adolescents treated with SSRI anti-depressant medications.[21]

The FDA statement reads as follows:

> Food and Drug Administration (FDA) asks manufacturers of all anti-depressant drugs to include in their labeling a boxed warning and expanded warning statements that alert health care providers to an increased risk of suicidality (suicidal thinking and behavior) in children and adolescents being treated with these agents, and additional information about the results of pediatric studies.[22]

For further information, refer to the National Institute of Mental Health's Web site on medication at: http://www.nimh.nih.gov/publicat/medicate.cfm#ptdep14.

Further Reading

The following books and Web sites are very useful in furthering your consumer research. Again we caution you: Be aware of the particular point of view the authors have. Their information is useful, but also comes with a bias. It is, in the end, your decision to make, and should be based on all the information you can get. Like a good consumer buying a car, you may know that there is a chance that the auto you are about to purchase comes with strings attached. Sometimes, even if it sparkles and shines and smells like a new car, you buy it and may later regret your decision.

American Academy of Child and Adolescent Psychiatry. Available online from http://www.aacap.org/.

Breggin, P. (1991). *Toxic Psychiatry*. New York, NY: St. Martin's Press.

Department of Health and Human Services. (1999). Mental Health: A Report of the Surgeon General. Rockville, MD: Department of Health and Human Services, Substance Abuse and Mental Health Services Administration, Center for Mental Health Services, National Institute of Mental Health.

Duncan, B.L., Miller S.D., & Sparks, J.A. (2004). *The Heroic Client.* San Francisco: John Wiley and Sons.

Medical Economics Data Production Co. *Physicians' Desk Reference,* 54th edition. (2000). Montavale, NJ: Medical Economics Data Production Co.

National Institute of Mental Health—*Teenage Brain: A Work in Progress*. Available online from: http://www.nimh.nih.gov/publicat/teenbrain.cfm.

Seligman, M.E.P. (1993). *What You Can Change, and What You Can't*. New York: Ballantine Publishing Group.

Seligman, M.E.P. (2002). *Authentic Happiness*. New York: Free Press.

U.S. Food and Drug Administration, Center for Drug Evaluation and Research. Antidepressant Use in Children, Adolescents and Adults. Available online from http://www.fda.gov/cder/drug/antidepressants/.

PART III: THINGS YOU NEED TO KNOW— ETHICS AND PAYMENTS

If you think that getting help for your concerns is a difficult activity, you are right. As a consumer, you really need to know about the small, seemingly unimportant parts of the complex system called mental health treatment. In Chapter 7 we will acquaint you with the codes of ethics that every clinician must abide by. Why should you know this? Because these are your rights as a consumer! Each year, dozens and dozens of clinicians are either given sanctions by their respective professions, fined, or worse yet, taken to court because they have violated the laws and ethical codes that govern the field of mental health (see Chapter 7).

How are you going to pay for the services you receive? Your insurance, *if* you are lucky enough to have coverage for mental health treatment, has limitations on services, and clauses are often included that are intended to keep costs down, rather than provide lengthy treatment for unspecified problems. You will understand the ins and outs of insurance and managed care after reading Chapter 8.

Finally, in Chapter 9, we will present a sophisticated and thoughtful set of alternatives to treatment that are not often brought up by clinicians, but useful nonetheless. Our "Spectrum of Services" as well as our list of questions you can use to interview perspective clinicians will ensure the best care for your particular problem, as an informed consumer.

Chapter 7

Legal and Ethical Issues: What You Should Expect As a Consumer

> We view clients as partners with their therapists in the sense that they are involved as fully as possible in each aspect of their therapy.
>
> Corey, Corey, & Callanan (2003)

Perhaps out of all professionals, mental health clinicians have one of the greatest needs for a code of ethics and laws governing their practice. These laws and guidelines are primarily for consumers' benefit, but they also provide direction when clinical relationships become strained, confused, or troubled. Your clinician will have intimate knowledge about you and be in a position to influence your decisions. This can have a lasting impact on how you might interact with significant others, understand your world, as well as on your trust *and* finances. It is an awesome responsibility and *the* main reason clinicians have guidelines and laws that guide and regulate them. Mental health clinicians are regulated by law at the federal level, as well as the state level, and are held accountable by ethical standards by the different organizations that train and accredit their profession. We shall go over each of these in this chapter. But first, I want to again make the point that seeing a mental health clinician should be guided by your informed consumerism, and the concept of *informed consent* takes into account all of the legal and ethical issues you need to know. Informed consent, like good consumerism, means that you are going about selecting and engaging in counseling of your own free will. It also means that you understand and agree to all that will transpire during that time and to how it may affect you afterward (see Box 7.1).

BOX 7.1
Something You Should Know

While teaching internship class, I always ask if students who have been in counseling were ever told their rights. As it turns out, almost all of the students have been in some form of counseling, and not one of them has had their rights explained to them, except for confidentiality. Informed consent was left out of any discussion by their clinicians.

Today, the use of third-party payers—insurance, managed care, and government contracts and grants—magnifies some of these ethical issues, making your life an open book to other people, besides your clinician. This is not always to your advantage, but like any other part of health care, is a necessary encroachment on your personal life and privacy if you are going to use insurance benefits. For this reason, you need to know about your rights, the law, and ethics involved in a mental health professional relationship.

In their book, *Issues and Ethics in the Helping Professions,* Gerald and Marianne Corey and Patrick Callanan point to *informed consent* as the most important element of an ethical practice.[1] An open relationship between you and your clinician requires an understanding of what is happening during your counseling and that it is performed with your permission. There must be, in almost every instance, voluntarily agreement to participate in the process of clinical counseling. Sometimes your clinician or his or her receptionist will give you a page or two of written information and have you read and sign it prior to beginning counseling. Some clinicians explain it all, some don't. Remember: it is *your right* to have it all explained *to your satisfaction* before you sign anything as well as at any time during your treatment.

An ethical practice begins with your clinician assessing your understanding of your rights. As logical as this seems, because clients come from different cultures, with different levels of education and understanding, or with a heightened state of anxiety, some people are unable to understand their rights. If you are stressed or upset, your rights may not make much sense to you at the time. Also, you probably will want to move quickly to tell your story or express your feelings, rather than listen to what your rights are. But it is your clinician's responsibility to make sure, over and again, that you fully understand *all* of your rights.

Informed consent takes in almost all of the ethical concerns and rights you may have as a client. The following checklist from Wheeler and Bertram will be used as a basis of our explanation of your rights, the ethical behavior you should expect, and the legal codes that protect you.[2]

INFORMED CONSENT

Voluntary Participation

In most cases, unless you have threatened to take your own or someone else's life and a psychiatrist has signed involuntary commitment papers, or a judge or a person using their legal authority has ordered you to go to counseling, your participation in counseling is voluntary. *You may leave at any time.*

The fact that you are participating of your own free will is a good thing. It means that you most probably have a strong motivation to work on whatever you can to improve your situation. It also means that you have been empowered to work collaboratively with your clinician—to take control and direct the course of your own counseling as well as you can.

Therefore, you must take responsibility for dealing with any of the issues you may have with your clinician in a responsible way. If you don't understand something, you have the right *and the responsibility* to ask questions, request more information, and work out disagreements you may have with your clinician. Unless you were mandated to seek counseling, sitting in that chair is something *you* decided to do. Even if you are required to be in counseling, you should take this opportunity to make responsible decisions and use your time wisely to work on important issues that affect you. You are in charge.

Client Involvement

You have a right to know what you will be asked and expected to do in counseling. You should know approximately how often and for how long you will need to meet prior to committing to counseling.

Based on the sort of dilemma you or your family might have, your clinician should be able to give you a ballpark figure about what he or she believes needs to happen and why, what you may need to address, *and along with you,* what signs of change you should be looking for that will signal movement to completion of this work together. Sometimes a clinician may give you a vague "as long as it takes" answer. These days that's not really good enough by clinical or insurance standards. By at least the third session, most clinicians should be able to provide you with a rough number of sessions or months you might need to attend, what sorts of issues you will probably want to address and work on, as well as how much of this will be paid by insurance as well as out of your pocket. The days of staying in therapy for years, and having someone else pay for it are over. If it is supportive help you need, rather than counseling/psychotherapy, there are other options we will talk about in the final chapter—all a lot less expensive.

Remember that your clinician isn't supposed to be working *on* you; you are both in this together collaborating during all phases of the work. However, there are many variables that might change during the course of counseling. Issues and challenges come up that can shorten or lengthen counseling, and new information may change the context of discussion. But each of these nuances should be discussed openly as they come up, with regard to how they impact your experience. You have a right to know what is going on during your own counseling experience.

You should understand what you might be asked to do and why, before it happens. You could be asked to talk about issues that you aren't ready to discuss, and you should know how your reluctance will be handled. Every profession has an ethical concern for clients' rights to self-determination. You will want to know how your unwillingness to talk about these issues will be interpreted by your clinician. Will he or she see this as your resistance to getting help, or will this be seen as your personal choice? If your clinician begins asking questions, or leading you into areas of your life that you don't feel ready to discuss, you should be prepared to ask him or her how this sort of discussion is related to the concerns that brought you into counseling. Your clinician should be prepared to, first, make a link between what they are asking you to do and your presenting dilemma, and second, be agreeable to giving you time to be prepared, or suggest alternative ways of arriving at the same outcome without the unpleasantness. Remember, there are multiple models of counseling, and they all have relatively the same chances of similar outcomes. Again, you, as the consumer, are in charge of your life and the course of your therapy. The old adage "no pain, no gain" is wrong!

In addition, you should know your clinician's reasons for asking you to consider medication or taking psychological exams. Your clinician should be able to make an intelligent link *that you agree with* between what they ask you to do and your reason for being in counseling. As we have discussed in previous chapters, counselors operate from different beliefs about what causes your dilemmas and what model will be helpful to you. Make sure they can explain their reasoning to your satisfaction.

A Teaching Vignette

Willa and her husband, John, a newly married couple, came to see me regarding a sexual problem they were having. Willa had a psychosomatic condition called vaginismus that prevented her from engaging in intercourse with her husband. I could tell there was something haunting them, but when I asked about it, Willa would shut down and become uncommunicative. John would try to console her and then start to explain something to me, but Willa would say, "No, no, please don't talk about it."

I told her that I would respect her right to avoid the issue for now, but that I hoped the three of us could discuss it sometime if it might help me understand their dilemma better. For two more sessions, Willa and John talked about relationship issues, and I kept my bargain by not pressuring her to discuss painful issues. Then, on their fourth visit, she said she was ready, and slowly began to discuss their premarital sexual experience that had led to an abortion, which their faith did not condone. Within a few more sessions, Willa and John were working on the forgiveness they needed from each other and well on their way to a healthy married life together.

By giving Willa the space she needed to get ready to talk about a very hard subject, she was empowered and allowed to make the choice herself. Willa had the right to talk about what she wanted, and it was my obligation to allow her to do so, as is her right to self-determination.

Counselor Involvement

What is it that your clinician will be doing with you, to you, or for you? Will they give you any advice? Will they only reflect your feelings back to you? Will they be looking for and amplifying your strengths? Will they focus entirely on your dilemmas, or want you to discuss your past in depth? Will they be active in the sessions, or will they be quiet, listening, and sometimes making comments or clarification. If you are seeing a hypnotherapist, or a clinician who does some sort of bodywork, ask specifics about how they will work with you, and about the potential risks. What about touch? Will they ever have physical contact with you, such as hugs, a friendly pat on the back?

If you are seeing a clinician because you were mandated to do so by a court of law, you will want to know if the clinician will advocate for you, write letters, or appear in person at court hearings. You will want feedback from your clinician on a regular basis regarding their perceptions of how well you are doing and collaborating on setting goals.

You should also know if they are going to direct your treatment or work collaboratively with you. As mentioned in earlier chapters, their model of counseling, and how they believe it will help you, will be a guide for them as to their own involvement.

A Teaching Vignette

Early on in my career, during a very charged, but important group therapy session, I learned a very important lesson about touching. The members of the group had worked through some particularly stressful issues with one of the women in the group. After the hard work, I congratulated the woman and group on the honesty and support that had happened in session, and went to lend what I thought would be a hug of supportiveness to the woman. She pulled back quickly, a scared look on her face, and said, "you are the first man who has touched me since I was raped last year." Now, she had never told anyone of the rape, but I had crossed a boundary I did not intend nor want to cross. She may have needed a hug, even liked it, but I learned to ask permission after this event.

What about more intimate contact or involvement? I have a colleague who starts almost all of her classes with a short lesson on ethics. She says, "Ethics. . . . What you *really* need to know is—don't sleep with your clients!" This short and to-the-point "lesson" says volumes about my colleague's biggest concern when training future clinicians. Why? Because sexual behavior between client and clinician is a problem—a serious problem—in the mental health profession, even though it doesn't occur very often. Having a sexual relationship of any kind with a client is an ethical violation of *every* profession in this field, and yet it occurs. Sexual relationships with clients are thought to be so unethical that several of the professions do not allow it for several years after the termination of the professional relationship.

Think about this for just a second: two adults in a room alone together, talking about the feelings that one of them (hopefully the client) has, and the other is an active listener, empathizing and showing concern. The purpose of the therapeutic relationship *is* to foster intimacy and trust. But not the kind that has potential for causing more problems. Reportedly, 87 percent of psychologists (76 percent of women and 95 percent of men) admit that they have had a sexual attraction to a client at least once during their career.[3] A study of sexual contact between nurses and patients in psychiatric hospitals found that 17 percent of the male nurses and 11 percent of the female nurses reported having had sexual contacts with their patients.[4] But it is not just about sexual acts. Any unwanted contact, language, or flirtations are inappropriate and you have a right to ask that it stop, and to report it to either the clinician's supervisor or to the state licensing board.

Touching is a very important part of human life, but in supercharged therapeutic relationships, if it is not wanted, or your clinician has not asked permission to pat you on the back or give you a hug, then contact is out of bounds. Sexual contact or suggestions are outside the ethical boundary line and can be grounds for legal and professional action.

Client involvement also means how, why, and when your clinician can terminate the treatment process. There are times when a clinician discovers that for one reason or another, continuing to see a particular client any longer, would be harmful or non-therapeutic. Impasses can occur, limits of the clinician's skills become apparent, or the client's inability or unwillingness to move further in the process can all bring the relationship to a halt. But, unlike you, your clinician cannot abruptly terminate the relationship and treatment; he or she must stick with you, work toward a mutually acceptable termination, or help find a replacement for services. To simply stop seeing you would be abandonment, and can jeopardize your health—and the clinician's license. Abandonment is not condoned in most organizations, and there is a process of transfer that must be adhered to or your clinician has broken not only ethical boundaries, but most often legal ones also.

No Guarantees

Because of the nature of all therapies, the uniqueness of each individual, and the fit with the particular clinician and his or her particular model of treatment—all which are necessary for excellent treatment—it is impossible to predict if the experience will be useful or not. However, as we said in Chapter 3, research has shown that counseling/psychotherapy works.[5] Regardless of the model your clinician uses, most clients improve significantly within six months, and over half will see improvement after only a few months. Also, if clients are active and a part of their own treatment goals, changes are more likely to last. Positive outcomes are related to your interest, involvement, hope, and working relationship with your clinician, as well as the seriousness of your dilemma. Most of the process success is because of what you do!

With medication, we know that there might be a lag between the time you begin and when the medication might take effect, and there are potential side effects, but they can be a life saver to many people. Some of this positive effect is related to our culture's belief in quick-fixes, however, and in some cases, just your belief in them can influence their usefulness. Remember, your degree of hope and faith play a large part of the success of any medication you might choose to take. But given all these facts, no clinician can ever give you a 100 percent guarantee that your life will be completely changed for the better.

Risks Associated with Treatment

Clinicians are obliged to discuss the potential risks involved with the particular treatment they are suggesting or providing. For instance, there is always a risk/benefit ratio associated with each medication, so your clinician should be able to tell you what percent of people using the medication are likely to have specific side effects, as well as the success rate for each. You have a right to know this information and to discuss it with your prescribing clinician.

Your clinician can and should be able to tell you what the likelihood is for you to benefit with the particular model of counseling he or she uses, as well as potential problems that might arise. Some talk therapies involve discussing and working through past traumas that could be difficult for you. There have been discussions regarding "false-memory syndrome," the idea that during counseling, a clinician's words may convince you that something has occurred in your past that really did not happen.[6] Like many mental health problems, sincere and competent professionals can assume positions regarding treatment and cite research that can affirm their beliefs. But there are risks associated with every form of treatment, and your clinician should be prepared to discuss them realistically with you, pointing you in the direction of both positive and negative views.

As a client, you might develop a strong attachment to your clinician, and your objectivity and ability to decide what is right for yourself might be compromised. The trust you have with your clinician should be weighed against your own research and common sense. Taking part in some form of mental health treatment means that you rely on someone else for information about your life, but also that you need to be responsible for your own decisions. If something happening in your treatment does not feel right, talk about it with your clinician. If you don't believe you are getting straight answers, do your own research, or seek a second opinion. It is your life and future, and as a consumer you have rights and responsibilities.

CONFIDENTIALITY AND PRIVILEGE

The cornerstone of any ethical practice is a client's trust. To ensure that trust, several professions that deal with highly personal and potentially embarrassing or damaging information guarantee confidentiality. You may have heard this in several contexts: "What is said here, stays here." This is the fundamental ethic that has guided such professions as clergy, lawyers, and physicians. It also is fundamental to every profession in the mental health field. But it has exceptions, and we will discuss those in the next section. For now, you can rest assured that what you tell your *licensed* clinician will be confidential, and is considered privileged information—not to be shared, as long as you have not done something illegal.

Confidential means just that. No one, except those within the context of the therapeutic relationship, such as your clinician's supervisor, office staff who file records, and sometimes your clinician's peers who may be asked for suggestions, will know what you are doing or talking about or even the fact that you are in counseling. Most likely, you will not even be named in these contexts, except by your first name. If asked by someone outside the walls of treatment, unless your records have been subpoenaed by a court of law, your clinician can neither deny nor admit that you have been, or are in counseling unless you waive your rights. All states have laws regulating confidentiality, and there is a federal ruling that upholds this right, except under the exceptions discussed as follows.

Privacy means just that. By law, your records are private. This information cannot be shared with others unless you agree to it, or a judge orders your clinician to disclose it because of a criminal act you may have perpetrated. So basically, your discussions within the therapeutic relationship are considered privileged communication and confidential. If you have any questions about confidentiality, you should talk with your clinician and ask him or her what confidential and privileged communications means to them.

A Teaching Vignette

Mr. Jones had two very difficult sons, David, aged fourteen, and John, aged sixteen. The Jones family had come to see me about the problems with their sons, which included extreme rudeness and failure to cooperate with adults. One Saturday, the family came in for their appointment and John had a huge red mark on his face. When questioned, Mr. Jones told the story of how John became physically violent, breaking furniture, and how Mr. Jones had slapped him to gain control. I explained my role as a mandated reporter. I suggested that we call the state Abuse Hot Line together and that Mr. Jones report his actions as well as the fact that he was sitting in their family counselor's office, so that the situation would not get out of control. He did; a report was filed but never acted on, and they were instructed by the authorities to continue their work in family counseling. It was hard for all of us to do, but it worked out for the best.

Exceptions to Confidentiality and Privilege

There are exceptions to confidentiality you should know about. If you waive your rights so that information can be shared with insurance companies or other agencies where you were a client, or if you enter into a legal suit against your clinician, your information may be disclosed to other people. Next, there are certain situations in which confidentiality cannot be guaranteed, such as during group therapy and during couples or family counseling. Also, if there is a child or adolescent in treatment, the limits of confidentiality are expanded to include guardians and parents. All other exceptions have to do with abuse of someone else, threatening to harm another person, or making statements that you are going to harm yourself. Your clinician is a mandated reporter and therefore is required by law to report to the appropriate authorities if you report current or past child abuse or elder abuse. Abuse can be physical or sexual, and, in some cases, mental abuse. Neglect of a child in your care, which will lead to serious problems later, may be reported. For instance, if you refuse to provide appropriate medical treatment for your child, your clinician may need to report this to the authorities. If you tell your clinician that you intend to harm someone else, he or she is required by law to report this to the police, and also to warn the person you intend to harm. This is your clinician's "Duty to Warn," and your clinician can lose her or his license if a report is not made.

Sometimes, clinicians worry that these exceptions to confidentiality may create a problem in their relationship with their client. It has been my experience, however, that your clinician will more likely be concerned about helping you, and will be a strong advocate for you. The things that might lead you to engage in angry or violent actions are usually the very issues you need to discuss in therapy. Failing to talk with your clinician when you are this upset can cause more problems, and create a situation in which the issues are not resolved. It is better to work with your clinician to deal head on with these sorts of potentially harmful situations.

COUNSELING APPROACH AND THEORY

You will want to know the process of counseling/psychotherapy your clinician uses before you start any counseling experience. Mental health clinicians are not allowed to work outside their areas of expertise. This means they need to have had the training and education for the type of therapy you need. Make sure that your clinician has that specific training before you proceed. If you want someone to help you with issues such as substance abuse, sexual dysfunction counseling, serious mental illness, sexual abuse, etc., make sure that your clinician has had specific training.

You should understand what he or she believes about counseling, and how she or he works with your particular situation. Will your experience be long-term, short-term, collaborative, intense, or laid back? You have a right to know what they believe. They should be prepared to tell you what they believe up front, but if they don't, then ask them what model or models they will use in your treatment. Different models and theories have different methods of treatment (see Part III), as well as different views about what will be helpful.

Ask about *your clinician's background.* You should know how long they have been practicing, what their degrees and licenses are, if they have additional certifications or training, and especially if they have worked successfully with others who have problems that are similar to yours (e.g., children out of control, phobias of grasshoppers, inability to maintain a job, etc.). Ask them if they vary their approach depending on the situation or use the same model for every person or family they see. If they say they are *eclectic or integrative,* ask them what they mean by that, and how they make choices. Although counseling does not guarantee a successful outcome, and not every clinician has success with every type of problem, you *do* want to know that your clinician is on familiar ground, and if this approach has been helpful to others in similar situations.

COUNSELING AND FINANCIAL RECORDS

As part of a standard procedure of care, your clinician is required to maintain records of your counseling experience. This includes records of your sessions, notes that provide a running description of your progress, and issues you have discussed and are working on, most likely a treatment plan that outlines both your personal goals as well as the therapeutic goals, and other information regarding your mood and motivations during sessions. Also, your file will have information regarding any past counseling situations you have been involved in, if you have signed a release so your clinician can obtain those records, any medications, a personal health and mental health history, family dynamics, and possibly even a personal history and family genogram (family tree) so that your clinician can look back and see how far you have come. It is just like a medical record. Your file may also include financial records about your insurance company, if you have an outstanding balance, if you are on a sliding fee scale, and other information regarding your care and payments. You have a right to see your file at any time and your clinician should help in going through your file so that you understand it clearly. Many clinics, however, will charge you for copies.

ETHICAL GUIDELINES

Ethics are the moral guidelines of behavior one chooses to adopt. Every mental health profession has a code of ethics that includes much of what we are including here, and more. Ethics are not laws; they are guidelines that each profession has agreed will be *standards of care*. However, if a clinician violates one of these ethical guidelines, he or she can receive a warning, be placed on a temporary suspension, or lose standing within that profession. When we were new members of organizations we were always fascinated by the list of members who had an ethics violation filed against them, as they appeared in the monthly newspapers of each organization. We would read the names, offenses, and sanctions, and wonder how anyone who had been so publicly sanctioned could ever get back to business as usual. However, even though ethics violation charges can be made against a counselor, not all of them are founded. Although each profession has different ethical concerns, common fibers or strands run through each independent code.

The therapeutic relationship and its components are defined so that dual relationships don't occur, boundaries are clear, and the expectations of each party are understood. The limits of confidentiality and privacy are outlined, and both legal and ethical considerations are clear. After you select a clinician, you can find his or her code of ethics on the Web site of the major organization they are affiliated with. Ethics are there to protect you.

LICENSING REGULATIONS

In most states, professionals need to be licensed in order to practice their profession. Licensing is a state requirement, and your clinician should be in good standing with the licensing division of the state in which you reside. Chapter 4 gives some idea about the different professionals and their credentials, which can look like alphabet soup sometimes. If you have questions about your clinician, and you have access to a computer and the World Wide Web, you can find out the information you need to know at your state licensing site. You can do an Internet search of your state's licensing board by looking for your state, and professional licensing or occupation board. For instance, in Illinois, the site is at: http://www.idfpr.com/ (Illinois Department of Financial and Professional Regulation). All we did was type in "professional state licensing" in the search engine's box and clicked on the "search" button.

At most sites you will see a section where you can find your clinician's name, credentials, and whether he or she is in good standing or has any violations or complaints filed against them. It is always a good idea to check to see if your clinician is licensed or not. If you were going to buy an automobile, you would probably check online to see if the prices quoted for a particular car are within the ballpark. You should be even more careful when shopping for a clinician. State Web sites have reliable information, so use them! If a clinician is not listed, stay clear of him or her, regardless of how "nice" he or she seems.

CREDENTIALS

We discussed credentials in Chapter 4 to a greater degree than we shall here, but we do want to emphasize two points. First, credentials are an indication that the clinician you are choosing has met the *minimum* standards for the type of service you see indicated on his or her references, business cards, etc. It means that they have passed through a gate-keeping process that relates to education and training.

Second, clinical work takes education and training (knowledge and practice) as well as sophistication and social skills. Research has shown that what is really most helpful in the therapeutic relationship are mature social skills. These social skills seem to contribute over and again to positive outcome no matter what type of treatment is used.[7] Interestingly, a good relationship is also a fundamental aspect in lowering the chances that a client will sue his or her clinician for malpractice.[8,9]

If you like your clinician and trust them, you will follow them almost anywhere and do what they tell you is in your best interest. This component of the therapeutic relationship has been shown to be true in many different contexts and research studies. It is what seems to make up a great deal of the positive healing effect, but also has a darker side. A clinician may please you, but have little to offer. As a consumer, you need to be aware of what is going on in your counseling experience and trust your instincts.

So, aside from the clinician's good bedside manner, what credentials should you look for? Well, credentials, as we have explained before, come in several shapes and sizes. At the grand level is the accreditation of your clinician's training program, such as that of the American Psychological Association (APA) for psychologists, National Academy of Social Workers (NASW) for social workers, and the Council for the Accreditation of Counseling and Related Educational Programs (CACREP) for professional counselors, etc. Graduation from an accredited institution guarantees that the training has met basic standards for the profession. But graduate school, as hard as it may be to get into, is just that. It shows that your clinician has the intellectual ability to muster through grad school, pass the tests, turn in graduate-level work, and most likely pass a comprehensive proficiency test. There is more to clinical work than just being smart.

At the next level are personal accreditations. A clinician may attain these, which demonstrate that they have (in addition to graduating from an accredited graduate program) passed a test demonstrating proficiency above or in addition to their graduate degree. These can be national accreditations which provide clinicians with a transferable personal statement that they have passed additional requirements and maybe a test that ensures the public they have an understanding of the skills and theories pertaining to their field. These accreditations show that clinicians have taken coursework in a nonaccredited program of academic excellence. Two examples of these include the American Association for Marriage and Family Therapy (AAMFT), which is an independent association that credentials clinicians who have obtained the required hours of clinical work and have been supervised by someone with specific training who has an Approved Supervisor designation from AAMFT. This national association stakes its claim on people who have passed through "hoops" and grants them "Clinical Membership," attesting to their quality of training. The American Association of Sex Educators, Counselors, and Therapists (AASECT) is another association that provides specialty credentials at a nationally recognized level. Both AASECT and AAMFT accept clinicians from each field, so they offer a different set of requirements.

Next are specific credentials for specific fields. For instance, psychologists can obtain a certification from the American Board of Professional Psychology (ABPP). The ABPP certifies that the clinician has demonstrated a high level of proficiency in a subspecialty, such as clinical psychology or rehabilitation psychology, among others.[10] Other fields may have similar credentialing venues, all of which provide another level of competency assurance for the public.

Licensing is the highest and most important level of credentialing, and all fifty states have specific licensing criteria for clinicians. Licenses are sometimes based on the criteria of the professional organizations that accredit them; however, some states, such as California, have lumped several of the groups together, requiring a common basis of skills and knowledge. Because states are responsible for the licensing of professionals, sometimes it is difficult to understand who to see, especially if you have moved to a state that has different requirements. Licensing laws have two levels, usually. One is called a title protection, which prohibits people from calling themselves by a recognized professional name when they do not have the actual credentials, education, and training. Psychologist, Licensed Marriage and Family Therapist, and Clinical Counselor are examples of this title protection. What this means is that only people with the training and education can call themselves by this protected name. The second type of level is called a *practice act,* which limits people from practicing specific activities. For instance, only medical doctors can prescribe medications in states where this is law. In some states, this practice has been expanded to other groups, if they have the required training, so that nurses and psychologists can have the right to prescribe psychiatric medications if they have passed the training required in that state. Professions that have this right in the various states will most likely advertise this so you will know who can and cannot engage in this activity. Likewise, a practice act can limit other professionals' ability to do counseling, testing, etc. (a practice act) unless they have had the required training. The psychologists' practice act limits these activities in Illinois, but also has a stipulation that a licensed professional of another kind is allowed to practice these activities, if their membership holds a license in the mental health field. These license stipulations guarantee that the professionals have been licensed, are legitimate clinicians, and have demonstrated proficiency in these skills.

Finally, there are many accreditations and certifications that professionals may earn to assert to the population that they have gone beyond the basics in their profession or subspecialty. It is wise to check out all of your clinician's credentials and understand what they mean.

A word of caution is in order here. Some credentials are nothing more than a political statement to the public that a certain behavior is a condition that someone or some group believes can be treated. Any group with an agenda can set up a national accrediting body to represent various sides of a professional debate. For instance, one group provides therapy for homosexuals who want to act heterosexual; another group maintains that therapists can and do cause clients to believe some tragedy in their life took place when it didn't based on behavior that fits a "typical pattern." False-memory syndrome, as well as the cause of homosexual behavior, can be hotly contested topics by groups with different views. These special-interest groups set up a credentialing system which lends them some legitimacy, even though they may not be recognized by any of the legitimate professional organizations.

FEES AND CHARGES

Counseling costs a great deal of money; all health care does. It is, however, a necessary luxury for most, and it costs insurance companies a great deal. You will be charged for the time your clinician spends in counseling sessions, but you may also be charged for time spent writing reports and for copies of your records if you ask for them. You should find out how much your insurance will pay in advance, and figure the rest as out-of-pocket expenses, because most insurers will have caps on the amount of service they will pay for. In addition, there most likely will be hefty co-payments involved. Discuss up front, the issue of finances during your first session. Find out your clinician's policy regarding sliding-scale payments, be clear about what you want out of counseling, and ask how long your clinician believes it might take and cost you. How your clinician deals with you concerning this issue will tell you a great deal about how he or she will counsel you. You want a straightforward answer to your questions, or at least an honest attempt to help you find the answer. Talk in a straightforward manner about money with your clinician, and if you can't afford the services, ask for a referral to a competent community agency where you can get the same or similar services for less. There is no sense in starting up a counseling relationship, beginning to do some work, and then realizing that you can't afford it, or that your family necessities will suffer. Good consumers talk openly about needs and costs. Remember that counseling, if used well by you, can help your ability to live, work, and be more productive. Find a clinician you can afford and whom you can feel confident about, set out a plan, and work diligently.

Some problems may be with us for the duration of our lives, but a good clinician will be truthful about *your* particular situation, and should help you set a course that will be productive. There are no silver bullets, no guarantees, and no cure-alls.

Insurance Reimbursement

Chapter 8 will help you understand and negotiate insurance concerns. Questions about who will be responsible for payment, how much will be paid, and for what services should be settled way before the counseling begins. As stated several times in this book, most insurance companies require large co-pays for counseling, and services are usually capped at a certain amount. This is no different than for any other reimbursement for health care. Insurance, or other sources of payment for services, cannot be expected to pay for unlimited counseling, as we will see later. It is always best to read any insurance contract material before you engage in mental health treatment, talk with a representative of the company, ask your clinician what he or she believes your policy or plan will provide for, and begin making a plan that fits within your means.

An urban myth reports that insurance or managed care companies have written clauses in their contracts with clinicians that limit the sharing of informed consent with clients. Most insurance companies see this as unethical, but you should check anyway. Insurance companies' refusal to provide proper treatment for you would cause a dual relationship problem for your clinician. The clinician is, in a sense, serving two masters—you and the will of the company that pays for your care. You should discuss this with your clinician and ask if they are placed in such a bind by your insurance company's policy. If you have some form of insurance paying for your services, check with your clinician to see if there is a clause in the contract with your managed care company restricting disclosure of your rights.

Responsibility for Payment

All parties should know ahead of time how much can be afforded, for what services, and what happens if *and when* insurance runs out. Nothing leaves as bad a taste in both the clinician's and client's mouths than a surprise money dispute. Be clear about who will pay and for what way ahead of time. Your clinician or his or her representative should discuss this with you and make all points very clear

DISPUTES AND COMPLAINTS

Clients have several avenues available to them through which they can file complaints about services or fees. The first and probably the most accessible way is to discuss your concerns with your clinician. It has been my experience that most disputes or complaints are directly related to basic misunderstandings between the client and the clinician, and that a straightforward, heads-up dialogue will clear up most problems. Two people can often drastically misunderstand each other when in the heat of emotion, or sidetracked with the basic day-to-day "stuff" that goes on. Most often, both parties can sense that something is wrong, but sometimes neither is willing to address the issue feeling that if they just let time pass, the issue will resolve itself or go away. Sometimes it does. When it doesn't, there can be a bigger problem than before, hurt feelings, and even anger, or at least major insecurities. Dealing with the issue right away, up front, and directly is *the* best way. The anxiety of bringing the issue up is most often worse than the discussion about it. Time can blow the problem out of proportion, like a balloon, until it explodes. Mature people who know better sometimes make bigger problems out of small ones.

If talking directly to your clinician doesn't work, ask for a meeting with your clinician's supervisor (if one is available).

Another approach is to contact the professional organization the clinician is affiliated with, and finally, the licensing board. All professional organizations have ethics committees. Your complaint causes the board to make a decision about the ethical behavior of one of its members, and no organization likes unethical behavior. It is never good to have an unhappy client (customer) saying negative things about members of an organization. It's simply bad public relations. The organization will collect data, investigate, convene, review, and make a decision that is felt to be fair. This is its role; most organizations take their responsibility very seriously.

Finally, every licensing board has an ethics board attached to it, which conduct the same sorts of investigations, deliberations, and decision making that the professional organizations do. They are usually made up of people from the profession who are experts at ethics and some concerned citizens who want to lend their time and community spirit to protect other citizens. Most licensing boards have a Web site where you can log a complaint. Look up your particular state and take a look, or call them.

Ethics and the law are good things to understand before entering into a therapeutic relationship. Just knowing that you have rights will help you feel more in control. Hopefully you will never need to file a complaint, because you will have chosen an excellent clinician after you have informed yourself with all the information from this book.

Cancellation Policy

Cancellation policies are very important to understand. Clinicians book their time with you and their time is valuable to them. A clear and understandable cancellation policy should be part of the clinical contract. We may all have times when events crop up that are out of our control, but you should be responsible enough to play by the rules. If you need to change your appointment, and there is a standard policy regarding cancellations, call or inform your clinician within the required time frame, or be willing to pay the consequences. Sometimes counseling can bring up issues you don't feel ready to talk about, but you should not use that as an excuse to miss sessions. It is far better to tell your clinician up front, and work on something else, than to short change the person who is trying to help you. Your agreement to participate and play by the rules is part of the relationship that will eventually help you out. If your clinician does not talk about a policy, ask! Make sure you understand all the pieces of your therapeutic relationship.

Affiliation Relationship

Many clinics, hospitals, and practices have affiliations with other organizations. These affiliation relationships should be openly advertised on you clinician's information. You might want to ask how these affiliations are related, and what their relationships to you and your work means. For instance, I once worked for a residential children's center that was affiliated with a larger organization. This relationship meant that when the larger organization was audited for compliance by our state's children and family services, the records at the residential center where I worked could also be audited. If this is the case, you need to be informed.

Supervisory Relationship

Supervision happens in almost every industry, so it should come as no surprise to you that your clinician probably has a supervisor who hears about how you, and others under the clinician's care, are doing. Clinicians who work *without* the aid and advice of supervision or consultation are foolhardy, as two heads are better than one. If your clinician has a supervisor, then you most likely will have a quality control working to ensure good care. Supervision is required by most agencies for new clinicians, as well as more seasoned clinicians, and in fact is a requirement for all professions to obtain licensure. Your clinician may have a supervisor who is appointed by the unit or agency where he or she works, or in some cases, your clinician may actually pay for his or her own supervision. Your clinician might discuss your situation with a supervisor regarding your care, and what he or she is discussing with you. Some supervisors will give suggestions regarding clinical work, providing an insurance that your sessions are thought out and fit standards of care. Supervision provides your clinician with objective feedback. Supervisors will offer guidance when your clinician might be "stuck," and give alternative views and suggestions.[11] You can ask about your clinician's supervisor and ask to meet him or her. Supervisors are required to adhere to confidentiality guidelines, just like your clinician, so meeting her or him and knowing that she or he is a caring and concerned person can help you continue with the trust needed to work hard during your counseling.

Colleague Consultation

Along with clinical supervision, most likely your clinician may talk about your situation with other colleagues. Sometimes they might do this anonymously, not using your name or identifying information, or if it is a close-knit office, they may discuss your care because others in the agency know about your situation and may have useful ideas that can help your clinician.

CONCLUSION

The laws and ethics pertaining to the field of mental health counseling protect consumers and ensure a standard of care that is not only helpful and careful, but that is universally accepted in a field where subjectivity and multiple ideas of helpfulness prevail. All of the points made in this chapter should be discussed prior to beginning your clinical relationship. Various clinicians and clinics handle this in different ways. Sometimes, clinics handle informed consent by having a receptionist give you a form that you must fill out and sign along with other paperwork prior to beginning your counseling. But at sometime during your counseling—most likely at the beginning—your informed consent on all these points should be covered. Your signature on a piece of paper, or your verbal nod, indicates that you understand all of your rights as a client, as well as the pros and cons of being in counseling. If you do not really understand all the pieces, you have not given your *informed* consent to proceed with counseling.

Chapter 8

Using Health Insurance to Pay for Mental Health Services

Always laugh when you can. It is cheap medicine.

Lord Byron

Early in life we humans realize that we are vulnerable. Young children fear monsters in their closets and other indescribable horrors. Older children learn that they may catch a cold from the kid in the next seat. Adults see car accidents and think, "That could be me." Seniors line up for flu vaccines.

This fear of illness and accidents is the essential basis of health insurance. Whether it's called medical insurance, disability income insurance, sickness and accident insurance, medical expense insurance, or accidental death and dismemberment insurance, health insurance is protection against financial losses due to expenses for medical treatment. This is a rational fear. Unpayable medical bills are a leading cause of personal bankruptcy.[1]

A BRIEF HISTORY OF THE INSURANCE INDUSTRY

As early as the seventeenth century, adults found ways to insure themselves against health-related disasters. By buying a little bit of insurance every payday, we can worry about other things. We can go to sleep at night without worrying about the accidents or illnesses that may strike us down before the morning comes.

By the late nineteenth century in industrial America, trade unions were advocating for better living conditions for workers and their families. In these industrious times, employers wanted to have "all hands on deck" when the day began. Illness and medical calamities were bad for the employees and bad for employer profits.

So, all over America, organizations began to offer families some protection against unexpected medical costs and services. In Texas, a hospital administrator named Justin Ford Kimball realized that many patients couldn't pay their bills. In 1929 he launched the Baylor Plan, which, for 50 cents per month, allowed teachers to receive up to twenty-one days of medical care in Baylor Hospital. This experiment flourished and evolved into Blue Cross and Blue Shield of Texas.

The unions across America realized that health insurance appealed to both union members and employers. Here was a win-win product that everyone wanted. Employers now paid the 50-cent fee as part of the remuneration package paid to employees. Over time, the benefit of health insurance became an expected part of the employment contract. On the surface this seemed—and in many ways was—a great deal for employees and their families. It also made employers into major purchasers of health care (see Box 8.1).

Health insurance originally paid for only hospital services. In the 1930s, insurance covered only the most calamitous injuries, accidents, and illnesses. It is difficult to say when health insurance benefits began to expand to include services beyond catastrophic coverage. It was probably as soon as two employers, hospitals, or unions began to compete for employees. To "sweeten the pot," employee benefit packages began to grow. Early on, physician office visits and prenatal "well baby" visits were added to benefit packages. This process, sometimes

BOX 8.1
Something You Should Know

What is a "benefit?" In insurance talk, a "benefit" is a service or product that is included (i.e., paid for) by the insurance company. So the benefits of an insurance plan include specific treatments by specific professionals, sometimes in specific places. Usually, benefits are listed on a health insurance "Certificate of Coverage," which people receive when they first register for a health insurance plan.

called "benefit creep," continues to grow the breadth, depth, and cost of health insurance.

By the late 1940s, as World War II came to an end and the Baby Boom started, the first hospital-based psychiatric facilities began to appear. At the same time, the concepts of psychology, psychiatry, and social work were beginning to penetrate into popular culture. Millions tuned into *The Bob Newhart Show,* the Peanuts character, Lucy, offered psychiatric help for five cents, and every college student read a few pages of Freud. Ever so gradually it became more acceptable to ask professionals to help us with our "personal" or emotional problems.

In spite of all this cultural enlightenment, the stigma associated with mental "illness" raged on. Even today, who among us would be willing to walk into our employer's office and say, "I am suffering with depression and I would like you to pay for my counseling sessions and my medications"? This stigma has slowed the adoption of mental health services into our increasingly broad health insurance packages. It took federal legislation, supported by hundreds of special interest groups, to pass the Mental Health Parity Act of 1996, which President Bill Clinton signed into law on September 26 of the same year. This act mandated that mental health insurance benefits must be comparable to medical and surgical benefits.[2]

Because the Parity Act is federal law, it directly impacts federally administered and funded health insurance programs including Medicare and Medicaid. For the Americans that have either of these insurance programs, mental health benefits now equal medical/surgical benefits. For the rest of us, who have commercial, nongovernmental insurance, we must wait for our states to pass equivalent laws that mandate equivalent coverage.

Since the Parity Act was signed into law, state implementation has been variable across the United States. For our purposes, it is sufficient to conclude that only eleven states have implemented parity laws without significant limitations to the scope or people covered by the laws.[3]

So what's the problem? you may ask. Most experts agree that there are two factors which explain why medical/surgical benefits are more extensive than benefits for mental health services. First, the stigma related to mental health problems is alive and well and flourishing in boardrooms and congressional offices across our country. Many people still believe that mental health problems are the fault of those with the problems. Second, there remains significant concern that the demand for mental health services could add significant costs to health insurance programs. Many people have emotional problems at some time in their lives. Employers fear that their costs will soar if health plan benefits cover all mental health problems and services.

In spite of the stigma and expected costs associated with mental health services, today most employer-funded health insurance programs include some benefits for inpatient and outpatient mental health services. Furthermore, medications designed to affect emotions and behaviors are now widely included in pharmacy benefits. The issues of limitations to benefits, such as the number of hospital days and outpatient visits with psychiatrists and counselors, and the patient's share of costs for services and medications, remain difficult and contentious.

Health insurance typically provides for services for our bodies and minds. While most Americans have become used to the limited choices of managed care, most would prefer to be able to choose the provider they want, whether he or she is a doctor, nurse, chiropractor, dentist, pharmacist, surgeon, nutritionist, optometrist, podiatrist, or a psychotherapist, to name a few. We want him or her to be able to order every possible test that he or she considers appropriate. We also want every treatment that is available. Finally, we want to be able to take every drug and dietary supplement he prescribed—or that we have seen on television recently.

Who Has Health Insurance?

In the United States, many adults with full-time jobs—and some with part-time jobs—have some type of health insurance. Specifically, about two-thirds of those with full-time jobs receive health insurance benefits.[4] If you work for a big company or governmental organization with more than 500 employees or if a union represents you, you are most likely to receive the benefits. If you work part time in a service-industry job, you are least likely to have health care benefits.

HEALTH INSURANCE AND THE MIND-BODY SPLIT

As we have said, most health insurance benefits include mental health services, also known as "behavioral health services" (see Box

8.2). Typically, health insurance companies "carve out," or delegate, the management services related to behavioral health services to organizations called managed behavioral health organizations (MBHOs). This division of labor parallels the historic Western division between the mind and body. Under this "split" paradigm, health insurance companies manage treatment for physical illnesses and they *delegate* the care of the mental health problems to MBHOs.[5]

The logic for this division of labor is simple: Health plans know medical care and MBHOs know behavioral health. In fact, most MBHOs were developed by forward-thinking psychiatrists who knew more about treating mental health problems than did the medical doctors and nurses at the health plans. Over time, many health plans bought the smaller MBHOs and brought the management of mental health problems in-house. Examples of this trend are found in such companies as Aetna, Cigna, and United Healthcare.

Is this a sign that the world is beginning to see that mind and body are connected? Maybe. In reality, managers of the health insurance companies think that they can save money by managing *both* the medical and the mental health problems. There are some significant functional overlaps in health insurance companies and MBHOs. Both must staff call centers, pay the claims of providers, and provide administrative support, for example.

Unfortunately, most of the insurance companies that own both types of services keep them separate in "silos" of functions. For example, the nurses that manage medical care have very little contact with the clinicians that manage the behavioral health care.

Whether the insurance company has an MBHO business partner or whether the insurance company owns the MBHO, the services

BOX 8.2
The Politics of Mental Health

Mental Health? Mental Illness? Behavioral Health? Psychiatric Services? Crazy? There are many different names for services related to emotional and behavioral problems. The insurance world uses the term "Behavioral Health." The reasons for this are unknown. We do know that this term refers to all types of human problems that are not obviously due to physical problems. This includes problems that have to do with behavior and problems related to feelings.

they provide are the same. Specifically, both provide the following services.

MBHO Services

Verification of Benefits

MBHOs maintain call centers for members or enrollees of the health insurance programs. These enrollees typically include the employee that carries the insurance and his or her spouse/partner and dependant minor children. The people who answer the phone are typically called customer service representatives or intake workers. These individuals are typically not licensed mental health practitioners, but they are skilled in providing information about the benefits of your insurance. In other words, they can tell you how much will be paid for what types of service and how much you will have to pay.

Assessment of Service Need

One of the key functions of MBHOs is to help enrollees determine the appropriate type of care that will help resolve the problems. For callers who already know that they want to see a counselor or psychiatrist, the customer service representatives usually just look up the practitioners who live nearby and provide names and phone numbers. They tell callers how many sessions will be paid by the insurance plan, the amount of the per-visit co-payment, and whether the plan requires that a deductible be paid before the full benefits can be used. When the caller requests a more intensive level of care, such as hospitalization, the customer service representative will transfer the caller to a co-worker who is a licensed mental health practitioner, usually called a "care manager." Care managers help callers determine if they need to be hospitalized or whether they need intermediate-level care, such as half-day treatment programs or daily outpatient visits. To make sure that care managers give consistent advice, they follow written "level of care guidelines." These guidelines synthesize the available scientific research on which levels of care best match which types of mental health problems.

Maintenance of a Provider Network

Most of us don't know how to find qualified mental health practitioners, let alone hospital-based services. For most people's problems, outpatient counseling and/or psychiatric services are sufficient. But MBHOs must also know the hospital programs that provide the best available care for people with a wide variety of mental health problems. Together, these practitioners and hospitals are known as the provider "network." The MBHO spends lots of money to recruit the providers, verify that they have current credentials and licenses, and to contract with them to meet service expectations in exchange for appropriate fees.

Linkage to Services

Using the contracted provider network described, MBHOs help enrollees access the care that they want or need. The MBHO's customer service representatives have access to long lists of practitioners in most communities. Generally speaking, only rural areas can have problems with having enough psychiatrists and counselors. Care managers know the hospitals and intermediate services (services between inpatient and outpatient levels of care) available in enrollee communities.

Care Management

Like doctors, lawyers, plumbers, and painters, mental health practitioners respond to the incentive of money. *Some* practitioners provide more services to their clients than are necessary because more services result in more money. Fortunately, mental health research and consensus among experts can be used to guide practitioners. This guidance, called "care management," infuriates many practitioners. From their points of view, they are immune to financial incentives and do not need interference by MBHO care managers, who are sometimes "below" them on the social pyramid of mental health practitioners (see Box 8.3).

BOX 8.3
Something You Should Know

NCQA: the Conscience of Managed Care: The National Committee of Quality Assurance is an independent, nonprofit organization that sets quality standards that shape the health insurance industry. By providing a variety of accreditation products and a standard set of health care data, the NCQA helps the public decide which health plans offer the best services and care.

Quality Improvement

MBHOs operate according to some general principles known as "quality improvement." Typically, a small staff of professionals lead projects to improve the quality of the company's customer and clinical services. While the details of these projects typically remain invisible to enrollees, they may occasionally notice faster answers to their calls, new written materials on common problems, more information available through the company Web site, and other such improvements.

In conclusion, MBHOs serve insurance companies and employers by knowing who treats what problems, and helping people get the services they need, when they need them. MBHOs relate to enrollees over the telephone through employee customer service representatives and care managers. They also maintain rich Web sites with information, sometimes in multiple languages, that provide another resource for problems and treatments.

Related Services

EAPs

In addition to the behavioral health insurance services, some employers provide a benefit called an employee assistance program (EAP). EAPs typically include services that are provided in or near the workplace. These programs tend to focus on interpersonal problems that directly affect behavior at work. The services provided by EAPs are usually brief and highly focused. Counseling services may be limited to six sessions, for example. In addition, EAPs often help companies promote healthy behaviors among employees, such as quitting smoking and avoiding workplace injuries.

EAPs also serve as an entry point for people with more complicated problems. For example, if I had a problem with my teenaged son, is this problem related to my work? This type of problem may or may not affect all of us, but, it can and does obviously affect our performance at work. People seeking help with this problem can be referred out by EAP staff. For one thing, EAP services are often completely free of charge for employees. EAP offices also tend to be geographically close to the employer.

EAP staff that directly provide services for employees are licensed mental health practitioners just like the counselor who has an office on Main Street. In addition, EAP practitioners tend to have knowledge of the types of problems that affect and/or occur in workplaces. For example, EAP practitioners tend to have extra knowledge of alcohol and other drug problems.

HOW DOES THE MONEY FLOW?

Health insurance companies typically have deep pockets and manage the benefits of a range of health insurance "products" or plans. They contract with businesses to insure the health of companies' employees.

In a very real sense, health insurance companies are positioned between businesses and their employees as follows:

Businesses → Health Plans → Employees

The employers buy health insurance products based on their overall value. Here is a simple equation that shows the relation between quality and cost:

$$\text{Value} = \frac{\text{Quality}}{\text{Cost}}$$

The purchasers of insurance products in the United States shop around trying to find the best-quality health insurance for the money. The biggest companies demand evidence of quality service and care from the insurance companies. When possible, purchasers use data to compare medical outcomes among the insurance companies that are competing for the contract.

Once the contract is awarded to an insurance company, the health plan manages the care of the employees and their families, collectively called "enrollees," according to the benefits chosen by the employer. The company employees consume the services and products allowed by the benefits and managed by the insurance company.

Our doctors and other care providers are the fourth parties in this system. These professionals provide the services and products consumed by the employees, according to the benefits set by the employer and managed by the insurance company. They typically have contracts with the insurance company. These contracts define how much the doctors and hospitals will be paid for which services.

The remainder of this chapter describes how employees and their family members can use their health insurance benefits to pay for mental health services. Specifically, this section will provide readers with the knowledge and skills they need to access behavioral health services through their health insurance programs.

ACCESSING BEHAVIORAL HEALTH BENEFITS THROUGH HEALTH INSURANCE

We have seen that there are multiple interests behind health insurance. The employers want to recruit good employees and keep them working. The hospitals (and doctors) want to get paid as much as possible. The employees want good medical care if and when they needed it. Unions want to grow their memberships by offering services that employees want. Savvy health care consumers keep these agendas in mind when they choose to access behavioral health services through their employer-sponsored health insurance.

Once the decision has been made to use health insurance to pay for all or part of the desired behavioral health care, the first step is generally easy. Find your insurance card, and turn to the side that has the more "fine print." Look for text that says "For Mental Health Services" (or similar text) and note the toll-free telephone number. When you have a few minutes in a private place, call this number. Usually, a customer service representative (CSR) will answer your call within thirty seconds. This person is a trained specialist but is not a licensed mental health clinician. He or she will ask you a few questions to determine that you are currently enrolled in a health insurance program and ask how she or he can help you.

The CSR will ask only for the general nature of the problem that you are currently trying to solve. He or she does not need to know your life history or even the details of the problem. The CSR's job is to help you get the services you want.

CSRs provide several specific services. These include:

- Confirm the benefits that your insurance program includes such as the number of counseling visits allowed per year, the amount of your co-payment per visit, and any annual deductible that you have to pay first.
- Provide you with names and details about mental health clinicians that you might choose to see for counseling or therapy. The CSR will be able to find several clinicians within a few miles of your home or business address. You will be asked if you prefer to see a man or a woman clinician and whether you prefer a clinician that speaks a language other than English.
- Provide you with names and details about psychiatrists and/or other professionals with the authority to prescribe medications.
- Approve or authorize you to use your health insurance benefits to get mental health services. Such approvals are becoming less necessary.
- Provide information on how you can access written materials about your problem or concern. Such materials are often provided through the MBHO's Web site and/or through a separate toll-free number.
- Record any complaints and appeals that callers have about the services they have received from the MBHO or specific mental health providers or hospitals. Some complaints can be resolved right away. When investigation and/or further intervention are required, the CSR forwards the complaint to the department that manages enrollee complaints.
- When a caller seems very unhappy or upset, the CSR can transfer him or her to a care manager who is a licensed mental health practitioner. Care mangers typically arrange access to hospital- and home-based services for callers that seem to need intensive care or services.

This process is typical for most enrollees. However, people in significant distress also have the option of going directly to the nearest hospital, doctor, emergency room, or other mental health clinician. These providers will call the insurance company, verify your benefits, and get approval to provide the needed services.

Common Problems and Their Solutions

In theory, the entire process works smoothly and easily. However, sometimes problems occur. Some problems are built in to the design of the process. Other problems have origins in human mistakes, technology limitations, and other factors (see Box 8.4).

The following are the most common problems encountered by enrollees of health plans who access behavioral health services through their insurance:

It Costs Too Much. The specialized services of mental health professionals tend to be expensive. For example, one fifty-minute session of psychotherapy currently costs between $50 and $150, depending on the geographic location of the provider. With health insurance, this cost is typically reduced to $10-$50 per session, which is typically considered a "co-pay." In addition, the insurance benefit may require that you pay a deductible before the discounted price applies. Deductibles can cost as much as $1,000 per year. Hospital services nearly always require that the patient pay the first $1,000 to $2,000 per year.

I Want More Than My Insurance Provides. A typical benefit for outpatient counseling is twenty sessions per year. In states where the Parity Act has been fully implemented, benefits usually include more than twenty visits; some health plans have no limits on outpatient visits. On average, Americans that use outpatient counseling attend seven visits. So for most of us, twenty visits is sufficient.

BOX 8.4
Something You Should Know

Balanced Billing: A Dirty Trick: Mental health providers and hospitals contract with insurance companies to provide their services for a preset cost that is less than the going rate. According to the contract, these providers cannot bill the patients for the difference. If a provider tries to "balance bill" you, let your health insurance company know.

Hospital-provided services are more strictly limited by insurance benefits. A typical annual benefit for hospital services is "x" number of days. For the few patients who require longer stays, the insurance may run out. This leaves the patients responsible for the costs of care.

I Want Something Different Than What My Insurance Provides. Managed behavioral health was developed by psychiatrists and adopted by medical insurance. Without question, this parentage has given managed behavioral health care more of a medical slant. Here patients have diagnoses—in addition to problems—and treatment often includes at least the suggestion of medication. Run-of-the-mill parent-child problems can morph into a diagnosis for the mother, one for the father, and one for the child. Problems of couples, which many marriage therapists consider to be "relationship problems," may have to be diagnosed as one partner's major depression before the provider can get paid. This "medicalization" of human problems and solutions will chafe for some.

My Provider Hates My Insurance Company. Many mental health providers blame insurance companies for their financial problems. In fact, many health plans have not raised their payment rates for many years. In addition, some providers think that they should be paid the full going rate. The insurance companies know one thing that some providers don't know: In most geographic areas in the United States, there are more mental health providers than are needed. Because the supply exceeds the demand, prices can remain stable. For every frustrated provider that quits, there's a line of providers wanting that person's position on the health plan's network.

I Want to Choose My Own Provider. Some people like to find their own providers. Some prefer one hospital to another. The problem occurs when the favored provider is not in the health plan's network. The result? The insurance company will either not pay for the services received or will offer to pay for less of the services.

All of these problems are real and worthy of discussion. As a health-plan enrollee you have the right to complain about these issues and more. When a plan makes a decision you don't like, you can appeal the decision. In either case, just call the MBHO, the health plan, or your employer and state your case. State regulations, accreditation standards, and the desire for positive publicity increase the chance that you will receive a fair and impartial hearing. If all of these channels fail, you can contact your state's department of insurance. These government organizations will further increase the chance that you will receive justice.

TOMORROW'S HEALTH INSURANCE

The insurance industry is changing every day. As health insurance costs continue to scream for the attention of the public and the government, health insurance products and services evolve to address cost and quality problems. Employers and government payers of health insurance costs demand ways to hold or reduce the cost of care for enrollees. Employees and their families are being asked to assume a greater portion of the costs that in 2006 reached $7,500 per person per year.[6]

Consumer-Driven Health Care (CDHC)

One trend that is worthy of note is "consumer-driven health care" (CDHC). This model of care is still being developed as this book is written, but it appears to be catching on. The idea is that Americans have learned to ignore the real costs of health care. If we could become more astute consumers, we'd learn to shop for quality and price in health care as we do when we buy a new television. We'd study our needs, ask around about good quality services, and compare prices.

CDHC insurance products tend to start everyone off with a small and symbolic pot of cash that is held in a personal account. This money can be spent to offset some of the out-of-pocket costs for office-visit co-payments, pharmacy co-payments, and more expensive and/or noncovered products and services. In addition, CDHC products provide tools to evaluate possible service vendors, understand treatment options, and promote compliance with treatment. Web sites, 24/7 nurse help-line services, and health promotion programs all help patients to be smarter consumers.

CDHC has not yet reached behavioral health care directly. However, MBHOs are working toward empowering consumers by providing information and services that help patients manage their own conditions. Most MBHOs have Web sites that provide hundreds of pages of information on identifying and treating psychosocial problems. Most offer extra services to patients with specific high-volume/high-cost diagnoses such as depression. One such program includes six weeks of mailed information on living with depression and monthly calls from care managers to facilitate treatment services. All of these services intend to empower patients to be smart consumers of behavioral health care.

CONCLUSION

In this chapter we have explored the complicated health insurance systems that can be used to fund mental health services. Health insurance developed and remains a benefit that employers fund in order to keep their workers functioning on the job. In fact, many employers choose not to provide this benefit, and many of those that do now ask employees to assume up to half of the costs of the insurance.

To make the most of the behavioral health component of health insurance, the wise consumer will understand the scope of covered benefits, access care within the network of providers and the included benefits, and know how to appeal decisions that are unsatisfactory. With the understanding of the limits of this method of funding, the consumer may find it to be a valuable addition to health insurance coverage and a viable way to pay for desirable services.

Chapter 9

Getting What You Need: The Many Alternatives

> Man has never made any material as resilient as the human spirit.
>
> Bernard Williams

> There is more than one way to skin a cat.
>
> Old Folk Wisdom

There is an old joke that goes, "How many psychiatrists does it take to change a light bulb? Answer—One, but the lightbulb has to really want to change." It might just seem to be true, after reading this book. The field of mental health is run like most of our health care system is today—those who usually need the services critically, such as the poor and severely impaired, have the most difficulty getting it, while those who need it least have better access (see Box 9.1). In much of the public mental health sector, the community agencies where the socially economically disenfranchised go, waiting four to six weeks and more to get an appointment is common, while the well-insured or private-pay client can be seen within twenty-four hours of deciding to seek help. The statement regarding children's (see Box 9.2) mental health is striking, to say the least. The statistics for adults are also grave. So, why in the United States, this great country, do we have such a dilemma? To answer that question, one must look at the way that our mental health system is set up, regulated, and funded. Let's review.

BOX 9.1
The Politics of Mental Health

Everyone knows the basic statistics: Forty-four million Americans have no health insurance. That's equal to the combined populations of Massachusetts, Alabama, Oregon, Iowa, Connecticut, Mississippi, Vermont, Arkansas, West Virginia, Montana, Louisiana, Indiana, Maine, and Nebraska. Fourteen states in all—every man, woman, and child off the heath care books. No other industrialized country would tolerate this. And the number of the uninsured keeps right on growing, along with the population. (*Source:* Barlett & Steele, 2006, p. 24)

BOX 9.2
The Politics of Mental Health

Some 15 to 22 percent of children have mental health problems that justify psychotherapy, but fewer than 20 percent of these children receive treatment. (*Source:* Kataoka, Zhang, & Wells, 2002)

In Chapters 1, 2, and 3 we discussed the three major models of how to understand your problems: biological, psychological, and family systems. But the deep-pockets interest groups of today want to see *every* human dilemma as biological, even when there is conflicting evidence to "prove" it. In Chapter 4 we discussed many types of clinicians, and that there is no evidence that one is a better clinician than the others. It has to do with fit—whom you will feel comfortable with and what you may need for your particular dilemma. Some clinicians have special training that can be to your advantage, but even so, fit seems to be most important. In Chapter 5 we walked through many of the different models of clinical talk therapy. Here too, as with types of clinicians, fit and basic people skills on the part of your clinician seem to be more important than the type of treatment they will use. In fact, some of those clinically trialed models show such good results because they are more amenable to research—they can be reduced to numbers and counted.

In Chapter 6 we looked at biological treatments, and in Chapter 7 we went over ethics and informed consent. Finding an ethical and open clinician is crucial to your successful outcome. In Chapter 8 we looked at insurance and managed care. Here you learned that mental health care is supposed to be on a par with other health care services.

Much of what runs mental health is determined by the notion that all of the problems people seek help for are lumped together as mental health (there it is again) problems in order for clients to be reimbursed or have their treatment paid for by a third party. This occurs so that clinicians can be paid for their services by insurance plans. The system all but demands that in order to be paid for services it has to be equated with a medically diagnosable disease or syndrome. Psychological and family problems all need to be diagnosed as medical health care problems in order to be paid for by health care dollars. This is a problem because not all mental health concerns are a medically diagnosable disease or syndrome in the classic biological sense. Some of the bio-psycho-social-spiritual problems are not addressed in the medical model of biology first. So how do you go about getting services that are shorter term, and focused on the whole picture? We will soon get to that as we discuss alternatives.

Because most of us are highly suggestible when we need help, or are in crisis, we will grab almost anything that makes us feel better. Because of this factor, it is important that you look critically at the hundreds of providers who want your business. Make no mistake about it, mental health service is a big business. The field is filled with clinicians and resources of every kind, ready to help you with the theories and strategies they want you to believe are just right for you. Hopefully, you will find someone who is open and willing to work *with* you, not *on* you, at a reasonable cost. With that end in mind, this last chapter will first present alternatives to costly and long-term counseling, a host of ways to find a clinician that is right for you, and suggestions about how to get good care at a reasonable price.

From the moment Adler, Jung, and Assagioli left the company of Freud, from the changing of the guard from psychodynamics to behaviorism, on to humanism, social psychology, family systems, and finally to biology, the field has been fraught with change. Mental health care has multiple views and truths. The current commotion is a repeat of what has been happening for the past century, as we only now begin to work together for the common good. But for some, mental health care is further away than it ever was from helping the masses. Medications are too expensive for the poor and often even for the middle class, as is quality psychotherapy. We have created a myth about people that discredits them with a problem-saturated view of life.[1]

Psychiatrist M. Scott Peck once said, "Life is difficult," and he is right.[2] However, by forgetting that life is *normally* a struggle, we have made more of the usual problems people have. By medicalizing them all, we have disempowered a generation. Kids are taught that it is easier to take a pill than to try hard, and parents are captivated with their ability to *give over the control* of their children to therapists and medications rather than have *responsibility for* them. We have seen parents who are so involved with making the almighty dollar that they have forsaken family stability, while other parent(s) have been so overpowered by their own drug and alcohol abuse that they abdicate their responsibility. Both are products of our culture. They are not real "medical mental health" problems, although we look to the "experts" to fix them, rather than to make changes in our society. Patients begin their medication only to stop it when they start to feel better, and the health care system continues to push its "one-trick pony" scheme. But this discussion is for another time. Now we would like to introduce you to our grand scheme of mental health services that we hope offers more choice.

SPECTRUM OF SERVICES AND PRODUCTS

The worldwide mental health industry has produced a wide range of services and products to help people suffering with psychosocial problems. These services and products include something for everyone in virtually every situation. Whether you're rich or poor, introverted or extraverted, worried about stigma related to mental health, there are services and products that will fit you and help you to feel better.

Traditional mental health resource lists typically focus on the services provided by professionals such as psychiatrists and counselors. Look up "mental health" in your phone book and you'll probably find only professionals who work in agencies and private practices. This is fine if you want to sit down with a specialist mental health provider and tell him or her your deepest secrets, but there are many other possibilities as well.

Imagine this situation. Theresa, a twenty-six-year-old, has been feeling blue since she gave birth to her first child, a lovely six-month-old son. She's having trouble sleeping and her husband thinks there's something wrong with her. If Theresa calls her insurance company, most likely she will be referred to a counselor or a psychiatrist. If she visits the self-help section of her favorite bookstore, she'll find dozens of books offering to help her solve her problems by herself. If Theresa talks to her minister, she may be invited to participate in weekly counseling sessions, referred to a women's group at the church, or given a pamphlet on depression produced by her church. If things look particularly bleak and Theresa walks into her local emergency room, she may be tested for thyroid problems and/or checked into the psychiatric unit of the hospital for a full evaluation of her problems. Or if Theresa happens to mention her sleeplessness to her primary care provider, she may get a prescription for a sedative or be told to find a skilled and sympathetic listener.

This situation has led many experts to proclaim that the United States has had a very serious breakdown in its mental health services. The mental health nonsystem has been called fractured, siloed, and dysfunctional. One of the worst symptoms of this problem is that many consumers don't know how to access the services that they need when they need them. This may be why only about half of all people with serious mental health problems get appropriate services for their problems.

This situation has been pondered for years. One possible interpretation is that many people ignore their problems and suffer in quiet desperation. In addition to these quiet sufferers, many people take their problems out on one another. Domestic violence, road rage, and workplace violence are obvious examples of personal problems that are not being properly addressed.

One thing is certain: All of these people have heard of psychiatry, therapists, and Prozac. So it can't be that they don't know that services are available. Some believe that the services would fail to help them. Some believe that they could not make the changes.

Some believe they don't deserve to feel better. And some can't afford it. We believe that the average person doesn't have a clue that there are at least ten distinct types—and thirty-two subtypes—of mental health products and services that have been helpful to many people. Granted, scientific research has not proved that all are effective or ferreted out which services are better for whom. Nevertheless, most of us have reasonable access to a broad spectrum of products and services, at least some of which would work for us for nearly every psychosocial problem.

One caveat before we go any further. There are hundreds of thousands of people in the United States who suffer the most serious and disabling forms of mental illness. These include major depression, bipolar disorder, psychotic disorders, and those who teeter between life and death due to suicidal thoughts and actions. These people and their families deserve help. They deserve treatment by professionals now, in environments that are safe and supportive. The Spectrum of Services and Products for Mental Health Concerns (see Table 9.1) shows the variety and value of these tested services (see column called Value).

People with the most serious mental health problems, their families, and the many other people that also suffer with mental health concerns, will find in the Spectrum a big-picture view of the products and services available.

In the rest of this chapter, we describe each of the types of services and products. We have included resources to help you find each type of service and product, as well as a lengthy description of some clinicians discussed in Chapter 4.

The Spectrum of Services and Products for Mental Health Concerns (Table 9.1) includes a rating for each type of service or product according to five dimensions including cost, ease, stigma, privacy, and value. These dimensions were chosen to correspond to the common barriers related to receiving appropriate treatment for mental health concerns. The definitions for these dimensions are as follows:

Cost refers to the overall relative cost for the type of product or service, compared to the others listed. Because of many variables, such as whether or not a customer has health insurance or happens to live in a community that provides free counseling to its residents, this dimension is only an estimate.

Ease refers to the overall comparative ease in getting this type of service. Criteria include transportation, the overall number of such services available, and the geographic distribution of the services.

Stigma refers to a typical degree of social stigma associated with the type of service or product. While the sense of stigma varies among us, we have attempted to rate each service in relation to others. Thus, psychiatric services are rated as having a higher degree of stigma than a self-help group led by a peer.

TABLE 9.1. Spectrum of Services and Products for Mental Health Concerns.

Service and/or Product	Cost	Ease	Stigma	Privacy	Value
1. Medication treatment/ management					
a. Primary care physicians	○	○	○	●	◉
b. Psychiatrists	●	●	●	●	◉
c. Advanced practice registered nurses	●	●	○	●	◉
2. Psychotherapy					
a. Individual	●	●	○	●	◉
b. Couple/Family	●	●	◉	○	◉
c. Groups	○	●	○	○	◉
d. Multifamily Groups	○	●	○	○	◉
e. Eye Movement Desensitization Reprocessing	◉	●	◉	◉	○
f. Neurofeedback	●	●	◉	◉	○
3. Coaching by professionals	●	○	◉	◉	○
4. Self-help groups					
a. Professional leader	○	○	○	◉	○
b. Peer leader	◉	○	○	◉	○
5. Health promotion programs and services					
a. Regular telephone contact and educational mail	◉	◉	◉	◉	○
b. Educational mail	◉	◉	◉	◉	○
6. Peer sponsors					
a. Face-to-face meetings, informal	◉	○	○	○	○
b. Regular telephone contact	◉	○	○	○	○
7. Social supports					
a. Family members	◉	○	◉	◉	○
b. Friends	◉	○	◉	◉	○
c. Church/Clergy					
i. Minister/Pastor/Priest	◉	○	◉	◉	○
ii. Stephen Ministry	◉	○	◉	◉	○
iii. Other peer ministries	◉	○	◉	◉	○
8. Holistic health care					
a. Exercise	◉	○	◉	◉	◉
b. Meditation	◉	○	◉	◉	◉
c. Vitamin therapy	○	◉	◉	◉	●
d. Diets to affect mood or behavior	○	○	◉	◉	●
e. Herbal medicine	○	◉	◉	◉	○

TABLE 9.1 *(continued)*

Service and/or Product	Cost	Ease	Stigma	Privacy	Value
f. Acupuncture	○	◘	◘	○	○
g. Other holistic approaches	○	○	◘	○	○
9. Psychoeducational events with professional teacher	◘	○	◘	○	◘
10. Self-help resources and/or publications					
a. Self-help books and articles	◘	◘	◘	◘	○
b. Web resources	◘	◘	◘	◘	○
c. CDs, DVDs, and podcasts	◘	○	◘	◘	○
d. Pathway to recovery workbooks	◘	○	◘	◘	◘
e. Journal writing	◘	○	◘	◘	◘
f. Recovery conferences	◘	○	◘	◘	○

◘ = Good, ○ = Fair, ● = Poor

Privacy is an estimate of the overall subjective experience of personal privacy that goes with this type of service. Services that allow customers to remain anonymous, like reading a self-help book, score high on this measure. Talking with counselors face to face scores low on privacy. Since all professional mental health services are confidential, this concept is not included in the privacy dimension.

Value is an estimate of the known relative effectiveness of the product or service based on scientific/research evidence, or expert consensus. Since mental health research results are always very narrowly related to specific problems in specific types of people, this rating is only a general guideline.

Borrowing from the easy-to-read format of *Consumer Reports,* each service and product has been rated on each of the five dimensions using a simple three-point scale—good, fair, or poor.

◘ = Good
○ = Fair
● = Poor

These ratings are based on knowledge of the research and clinical experiences. However, it was more difficult to assign these ratings than we expected. First, every rating is necessarily subjective and relative. For example, the per-unit cost of seeing a psychiatrist is high relative to every other service listed. So, we rated this cost as poor meaning less affordable than the other services. But the known value of psychiatric services has been firmly established by research. Research supports that medications prescribed by psychiatrists can be among the best practices for depression, anxiety disorders, and many other mental health concerns. So if you read across the row for psychiatrist-provided medication treatment/management, you'll see a poor rating for cost and a good rating for value.

MEDICATION TREATMENTS AND MANAGEMENT

As we have discussed, many of the most common mental health concerns can be effectively treated with traditional Western medications prescribed by doctors and nurses with legal prescribing authority. Sometimes called psychotropics or psychiatric medications, medications that affect feelings and behavior are widely and effectively used. For many mental health concerns, there are FDA-approved prescription medications that can help.

The medications used to treat mental health concerns are prescribed by three major groups of practitioners. Because the costs, ease, stigma, privacy, and value dimensions vary across these types of practitioners, each is described as follows.

Primary care physicians. Primary care physicians (PCPs) are medical doctors that provide general and preventive medical care. Formerly known as general practitioners or GPs, this medical nonspecialty was reinvented by managed care companies that recognized the need for a single doctor to coordinate all of the specialty care that some patients require. Today, PCPs include family physicians, internists, pediatricians, some gynecologists and obstetricians, certified physician's assistants, and others.

Americans flock to the offices of their PCPs in droves, driven by their health insurance and their need to have one trusted "guru" on all things health related. Perhaps because this office delivers nearly perfect privacy, and because crying babies, creaky senior citizens, and calendars with drug names shriek, "This is Medical Land," people suffering with every possible mental health concern also pour into the offices of these busy doctors.

In spite of the fact that PCPs typically see between four and six patients an hour, they provide care for the majority of patients with mental health concerns. These doctors, many of whom had only two to four weeks of education in psychiatry, somehow manage to listen quickly and to hear mental health problems obscured by aches and pains. Not surprisingly, because PCPs are the front line of mental health services in America, they prescribe the majority of psychotropic medications (e.g., 40 to 60 percent of all antidepressants) and the majority of hours spent listening to people in emotional pain.

Psychiatrists. Psychiatrists are the recognized medical specialists who are licensed to use medications to treat mental health concerns. All psychiatrists are physicians who have completed college, medical school, and a residency in psychiatry. Some have also completed a fellowship in a subspecialty such as child and adolescent psychiatry.

Psychiatrists typically practice in office suites that are dedicated to providing care for people with mental health concerns. These offices may include a family therapist, social worker, or a psychologist, but psychiatric practices are rarely integrated into offices with other *medical* specialists. Instead, their office doors read, "Psychiatrist," and therefore scare away many people who fear being seen in a "shrink's" office by a neighbor.

Advanced practice registered nurses. According to the American Nurses Association (ANA), advanced practice registered nurses (APRNs) are registered nurses who have also completed advanced educational and clinical practice.[3] Although Nurse Practice Acts vary widely, the majority of states give prescriptive authority to master's-level clinical nurse specialists who have been certified in psychiatric-mental health nursing by the ANA. This allows APRNs to prescribe and manage psychotropic medications.[4]

APRNs practice in general medical settings and in specialized mental health offices. For this reason, and because they can be known as "my nurse," they do not suffer the entire stigma that is unfortunately tied to psychiatry and psychiatrists. This may explain, along with the shortage of psychiatrists in some geographic areas, why APRNs are prescribing and managing an increasing share of psychotropic medications in the United States.

PSYCHOTHERAPY

Psychotherapy, in all of its many forms, is one of the most widely used treatments for mental health concerns. All over the United States, people file into the offices of counselors and therapists of every professional type. These offices, like those of psychiatrists, are normally distinct from medical offices and clinics. They are found on main streets and in multiuse offices, they may be in rooms in larger social service organizations, hospitals, prisons, large employers, and courthouses. Like psychiatrists, the doors bear words like "counseling center" and therefore scare off potential customers concerned by the stigma of seeing a "shrink." As this is written, it seems that the stigma interferes more with psychiatry than with psychotherapy (see Box 9.3).

Psychotherapy is a professional service that is paid for using discretionary cash, credit, state or federal money, charitable funds, or health insurance benefits. The providers of psychotherapy are generally licensed by the state in which they practice as any of many eligible professions including social work, counseling, marriage and family therapy, psychology, and others. Regardless of the license, most professionals provide psychotherapy for individuals, couples and families, groups, and multifamily groups. Each of these subtypes is listed separately in the Spectrum (Table 9.1) because there are more salient differences among these types of counseling than among the types of professionals that provide the services.

One significant difficulty with accessing psychotherapy is that most people don't know how to choose a good counselor. For more information on this issue, see Chapter 2 and later in this chapter.

BOX 9.3
The Politics of Mental Health

What's in a Name? Psychotherapy? Counseling? Therapy? Counselor? Therapist? In this section, we use the fancy term psychotherapy to include mental health-related therapy and counseling. In our opinion, the differences among these words are differences among words, only. The same can be said for therapist and counselor. While state licenses restrict use of certain terms or titles, where talk therapy is concerned, almost everyone speaks the same language.

Individual counseling. In individual counseling, the counselor and consumer meet together for forty-five to fifty minutes per week and discuss the concerns that the consumer presents. This is the most private form of counseling and therefore it is highly personal and intimate. Many people find this intimacy to be frightening, particularly at first. Some find it to be just too personal.

Couples/family counseling. Some counselors prefer to work with couples and families for two reasons. First, they believe that most, if not all, mental health concerns have powerful family and/or interpersonal forces at work that build, maintain, and solve human problems. Second, they believe couples and families working together during counseling sessions are able to learn by doing. This makes couples/family work efficient and productive.

Couples and family counseling sessions can be less threatening to some people. After all, the focus can't stay on one person for long. Plus, it can be easier to think of one's problems as family problems rather than as personal problems. In some social circles, it's cool to have a crazy family.

Group counseling. Group counseling typically involves six to ten people with similar mental health concerns. Many such groups meet once a week, like other forms of counseling. Because groups require people with similar concerns, it can be difficult for counselors to assemble a sufficient number of people for all but the most common problems such as divorce, depression, and substance abuse.

The cost of group counseling is typically far below the going rate for individual or family therapy. However, for some unknown reason, group counseling is not commonly included in insurance benefits. So, the weekly cost might be $35 instead of the $125 per individual session, but insurance might cover all but $25 of the individual session and none of the group session. The exception to this is that group counseling is often included in hospital-based services.

The stigma associated with group counseling is difficult to appraise. Groups are often held in counseling offices, so this involves some exposure. In the typical group, members take turns in the spotlight while learning through the attention to and experiences of others. This can produce a comfortable amount of personal privacy for people who don't appreciate too much close attention. On the other hand, a group participant can expect to be observed by and given feedback from other group members as well as the therapist. In addition, group members are not legally bound to confidentiality.

Multifamily group counseling. In multiple family groups, three to five families attend and share their experiences and help one another, with the guidance of a professional. As with group counseling, the barrier here is in assembling multifamily groups for less common problems. Hospitals that specialize in treating less common problems, such as eating disorders, can assemble multifamily groups more easily than can a private counseling office or community clinic.

Neurofeedback. Neurofeedback is a technique that is said to reshape and reprogram specific brain wave patterns that are associated with attention-deficit/hyperactivity disorder (ADHD). Neurofeedback uses computers and specific programs that present gamelike functions and sense brainwave activity. The patient wears a headset with sensors that affect the activity on the computer screen. Neurofeedback helps people improve attention through a trial and error process. Proponents of this treatment state that neurofeedback can change brainwave patterns associated with ADHD. Cost is similar to that of psychotherapy and is not typically covered by health insurance benefits. A wide variety of people hold certificates in the practice of neurofeedback but it is not available in all geographic areas. The evidence on the effectiveness of this technique is largely anecdotal.

Eye movement desensitization reprocessing (EMDR). Developed by psychologist Francine Shapiro, EMDR has become a widely accepted and well-researched technique used to treat acute stress disorder and post-traumatic stress disorder. EMDR uses a variety of techniques to promote active eye movement while the clinician instructs the patient to recall traumatic events. Through this process, the troubling memories are changed so that they have less intensity.

This procedure typically costs the same as a standard therapy session and is usually provided by clinicians who have been trained and certified in the technique. This approach may appeal to people who feel uncomfortable talking about their problems since the technique does not require disclosure of personal details. More information on EMDR can be obtained from the EMDR Institute, Inc. at www.emdr.com.

COACHING BY PROFESSIONALS

Coaching has become a potent source of help for some people. Coming from a combination of self-help gurus and leadership and/or business consultants, coaching provides people who can afford the service a way to get specific motivational help that is not considered therapy or counseling. However, many of the people who provide coaching do have graduate degrees in the mental health field and have begun to practice coaching as a means to help people to avoid the hassle of dealing with the managed care or insurance industry and potential litigation because they call their services "coaching" rather than counseling or therapy. According to the International Coach Federation (ICF), professional coaching provides:

> . . . an ongoing partnership designed to help clients produce fulfilling results in their personal and professional lives. Coaches help people improve their performances and enhance the quality of their lives. Coaches are trained to listen, to observe and to customize their approach to individual client needs. They seek to elicit solutions and strategies from the client; they believe the client is naturally creative and resourceful. The coach's job is to provide support to enhance the skills, resources, and creativity that the client already has.[5]

To those trained in the major fields of mental health clinical work, this sounds identical to what many licensed professionals do. This is true, especially today, with the current focus on strength-based mental health counseling (see Chapter 3). Coaches are not, however, licensed, nor do they claim to be doing clinical work. Because they do not claim to do clinical work, they don't need to be licensed, hold liability insurance, nor are they required to go through accredited schools of higher learning in programs that have standards adhering to these accrediting bodies.

Coaching professionals meet with their clients in an ever-expanding vista of alternative places such as online, by e-mail, over the phone, through audio- and videotapes, as well as in person. Coaching began as a motivational and goal-oriented service for business professionals to help them increase their personal goals and financial rewards. Many executives have found the help they need from coaches who help them set and attain goals, and stay motivated. Motivational speakers are also coaches, in that they may help provide short- and long-term goals for their clients during speaking engagements, and through the marketing of motivational video- and audiotapes. Most people are not self-starters, have a difficult time staying focused, and tend to lose the edge they need even after serious interventions. Coaches provide that kick in the pants to help people attain business and personal goals—much like athletic coaches who provide a game plan for their players.

Although clinical therapy has moved on to a shorter-term and quicker intervention strategy indicated by the health care industry, coaching now provides the potential for many to engage in expensive, longer-term contact without the constraints usually associated with health care.

SELF-HELP GROUPS

Substance abuse treatment programs rely on peer-group intervention and support, which has given birth to a whole cottage industry. Today, there are self-help groups for everything from being an adult child of an alcoholic, to those who have irritable bowel syndrome, to support for the bereaved owners of recently deceased pets, and more. For a more complete list, you could go to the American Self-Help Group Clearinghouse at http://www.selfhelpgroups.org where you will find listings of any and all potentially useful places to go for help and support. There are even Web sites that will help you start your own support or self-help groups.[6]

The process and concepts of self-help groups are easy to understand; groups of like-minded folks who have a wealth of knowledge about what works and what doesn't can provide new members with a potpourri of tried-and-true interventions, as well as anecdotal information about which professionals are helpful and which are not. Some of this translates to who is in the "club" and who is not; for instance at any Alcoholics Anonymous (AA) meeting, one can be instructed about who in the field "knows" about treatment from a program model.

This sort of information can be very useful in steering people away from making wrong moves and associations, but it can also limit the choices to treatments that fit with others' expectations of what is appropriate treatment, and cancels out other perspectives. For instance, many AA folks believe that the best treatment for substance abusers is one that includes only a twelve-step approach, nothing else or by no one else. Yet, research on this subject has demonstrated greater successful outcomes when twelve-step programs are combined with intensive family treatments.[7,8]

The bottom line is that self-help groups can be a wonderful step to getting help. They are usually full of interested and helpful folks who have "been there" and who are more than willing to listen to your concerns and point you in the direction of getting out from under whatever dilemma you may have. But, when the self-help group begins to become bigger than life for you (and this does happen), and it begins to set rules for "the best way" that you should get treatment, and its rules and regulations can become more debilitating and controlling rather than healing and liberating. Then, it's time to move on.

HEALTH PROMOTION PROGRAMS AND SERVICES

Since 1985, health insurance companies and some state Medicaid and Medicare programs have developed a new model of health care delivery called disease management or health promotion. These innovative programs are designed to help people with chronic illnesses while managing the costs associated with their care.

The Disease Management Association of America, established in 1999, defines disease management as "a system of coordinated health care interventions and communications for populations with conditions in which patient self-care efforts are significant."[9] Disease management or health promotion programs are shaped by the science on the best-known treatment for a particular disease. They use a combination of strategies, including mailed educational materials focused on helping people live with their illnesses, ongoing nurse telephone coaching of program enrollees, and monitoring of health status indicators such as blood-sugar levels. In addition, the most advanced health promotion programs direct members to providers with exceptional skills in the treatment of the disease.

The most common health promotion programs focus on the high-risk/high-cost medical conditions of diabetes, asthma, congestive heart failure, obesity, and back pain. In addition, managed behavioral health organizations have implemented programs for people suffering from major depression, substance abuse, and attention-deficit/hyperactivity disorder.

We have included health promotion programs on the Spectrum because they promote best practices in the few mental health conditions that they reach. The nurses that interact with the program enrollees are typically knowledgeable, supportive, and equipped with resources to help. Materials distributed to program enrollees tend to be high quality in content and appearance. Because these programs are free to people with health insurance—and some state-managed care programs—and reach individuals in the privacy of their homes, they score high on cost, ease, stigma, and privacy.

The evidence on the effectiveness of these programs is mixed. Some studies have shown that specific programs have improved the health of enrollees and other studies have found that other programs have not worked at all. As work continues on this interesting health care specialty, we expect that the evidence for its value will improve.

PEER SPONSORS

The Alcoholics Anonymous twelve-step-type program contributed another type of service to the Spectrum, peer sponsors. We include this as a separate service because the peer sponsor idea has jumped from its home in AA to other forms of mental health concerns.

Peer sponsors are typically people with the same mental health concern as the people they sponsor. What gives them the right to formally serve as sponsors is that they have lived with the concern for a longer period of time and demonstrated that they have managed the concern in an admirable and healthy manner. Peer sponsors volunteer their time and wisdom, and no authority figure assigns them to sponsor anyone. The member elects or chooses the sponsor and the sponsor serves at the member's pleasure.

Peer sponsors have proven their worth to thousands and thousands of recovering alcoholics and people with other addictive behavior problems. The wisdom of another human being who has "walked in your shoes" can be supremely valuable. At its best, the sponsor-member relationship is highly personal and in many ways intimate, like a long-term friendship. Like friendship, some peer sponsor meetings occur in informally face to face and others occur by telephone only.

The Spectrum rates peer sponsors as "good" on cost, since a sponsor's services are typically free. Peer sponsors can be difficult to find, depending on the sophistication of the self-help organization that serves people with your mental health concern. Peer sponsor programs, however, can be found (or created) in support groups established by any organization including hospitals, churches, and mental health centers. This earns peer sponsors a rating of "fair" on ease. We have scored stigma and privacy as "fair," because family and friends often know that the guy you meet for coffee on Thursday mornings is a special kind of friend. This is often a terrific sign that you're working with your condition rather than hoping it will miraculously disappear. Finally, because the value of peer sponsors has not been adequately researched, it receives a score of "fair" for value.

SOCIAL SUPPORTS

Family members and friends. One of the most important social supports for people and families in crisis is other family members and friends. It is to these people we most often turn for advice and support. However, when a problem or dilemma occurs, one of two events may also happen. In a family where there isn't openness and unconditional caring, the person experiencing the dilemma may try to talk about it with their significant others, all to no avail, most often because these people have some stake in the problem, even unwittingly. Like the old "elephant in the room" that no one talks about, some families become extra careful to make sure there is no talking, and no action to resolve the dilemma. Under theses conditions, the problem, like a balloon filling with water, can eventually split, break, and soak all who are around. Some families keep all personal information within the family structure, even when the situation is getting worse. "Not in our family," "We take care of our own," and "Our family doesn't wash our 'dirty laundry' in public" are all rules some families adopt.[10] This sort of behavior occurs often in families where there have been years of hiding secrets, or cultural prohibitions of talking outside the family structure.

In the second type of family the exact opposite is true. Support and concern increases the likelihood that a positive outcome will come about more quickly. Research shows that supportive families and friends increase the odds of positive outcomes. In fact, many people improve significantly without the help of formal psychotherapy in any form, pointing to the fact that significant people in one's life, such as family, friends, and the clergy, provide the support and hope needed to rise above and move on without formal care.[11] Clients who have positive relationships with their family and partners have better outcomes in their treatment.[12]

Places of worship and clergy. There is a reason why the clergy in many places of worship have had education and training in counseling. Clergy have been primary agents of help since the beginning of time. The early Western churches viewed people's problems as being the result of sinful behavior; clergy were seen as people who could straighten out the problems through prayer and righteous living. As we became more scientifically oriented, we found other reasons for our problems. But the clergy, for many, remain the first line of prevention and defense for mental health problems. Today, many clergy spend a great deal of their time counseling parishioners and members. The use of lay ministers in churches has relaxed the extent to which an ordained clergyperson needs to be involved with longer-term counseling. Clergy may suggest that people who are in need be seen by some of these lay ministers.

Stephen Ministry and other peer ministries. Stephen Ministry originated from Lutheran pastor Dr. Kenneth C. Haugh, who is also a clinical psychologist. He saw the need for lay ministers to help congregants when they had crises or specific problems that were not serious enough to seek professional help. Today, Stephen Ministry is in 9,000 congregations in more than 100 Christian denominations. Over 450,000 people have been trained as Stephen Ministers through an intensive fifty-hour training and follow-up of twice-a-month supervision and continuing education. Stephen Ministries have provided care for more than one million people, including help for the bereaved, hospitalized, terminally ill, separated, divorced, unemployed, relocated, and others facing a crisis or challenge.[13]

HOLISTIC HEALTH CARE

According to the *American Heritage Dictionary,* holistic is defined as, "An approach to medical care that emphasizes the study of all aspects of a person's health, including physical, psychological, social, economic, and cultural factors." Thus, holistic mental health attempts to treat mind, body, and spirit as a single system rather than as parts. They might also be called, as Dr. Andrew Weil says, alternative medicines, meaning "different from the usual or conventional."[14] There are several alternative or holistic means by which some mental health problems are treated. According to the United States Department of Health and Human Services Substance Abuse and the Mental Health Services Administration (SAMHSA), alternative approaches have a long and somewhat controversial history.[15] According to SAMHSA's Web site, the list includes such interesting alternatives as self-help, diet and nutrition, animal-assisted therapies, expressive therapies, art therapies, dance and movement therapies, acupuncture, yoga, meditation, Native American ceremonial dances and chants, relaxation and stress reduction, biofeedback, guided imagery, and electronic communications such as e-mail and telephone counseling. Called either "complementary or alternative medicines," clinicians may use these treatments, many of which are thousands of years old, in addition to more traditional forms of care. For instance, it is rather common these days to see a dance or movement therapist who is also a licensed professional working with clients using movement or dance as a vehicle to help clients get "in touch" with their lives and increase their successful outcome to better living.

Herbs have always played a part in health care, and such is the case in mental health. Many medicinal treatments have been used for centuries for such problems as depression (St. John's wort),[16] calming the nerves (passion flower),[17] or sleep aids (kava kava).[18] Many people would rather use what they consider to be a natural product, such as herbs, than a pharmaceutical product.

For a more complete list and understanding, consult the National Center for Complementary and Alternative Medicine Web site: http://nccam.nih.gov.

PSYCHOEDUCATIONAL EVENTS WITH PROFESSIONAL TEACHERS

For every problem known to human beings, there's someone who knows more about it than the typical person who has the problem. If the problem has been known for a while, there are probably books, magazine articles, episodes of *Oprah,* and several PowerPoint presentations on the topic floating around on the Web. If you look a little further, you'll find an expert who's willing to give you a talk about the mental health concern. Across health care, these services and products are called psychoeducation.

Psychoeducational events are for the people who are willing to find an expert—or at least a good teacher/speaker—and sit in a folding chair for several hours and listen. In addition to all of the written material you can find through the Internet or a trip to the library, it's often nice to have an expert pull it together and present it to you. Experts know what to emphasize, what seems to work best, and what's new on the horizon, all of which can be difficult to find on your own. We emphasize here that this teacher is a professional, rather than a peer. While peer speeches can be informative and inspiring, and written materials can deliver lots of information, we consider them different and discuss them as follows.

Good psychoeducational events include general information about the illness or concern, information on how it is best treated, coping strategies and problem-solving skills, and how to recognize signs of relapse and/or treatment failure. As group members listen, they contribute, enriching and personalizing the information. Teachers invite participants to express their needs and doubts and question the basis for treatments. Through this give-and-take, teachers encourage participants to see how they can be active in choosing, implementing, and evaluating their own treatments.

Hospitals and large public mental health programs sponsor most psychoeducational events on mental health topics, and the events tend to be free. Community newspapers and libraries include announcements of these events in their community calendars. We recommend calling local psychiatric hospitals first, but news of such seminars tends to spread quickly, so the local public mental health or family services office will also know about the events. Consumer advocacy groups such as NAMI and the Bipolar and Depression Support Alliance also sponsor psychoeducational events including recovery conferences, which are described in the next section.

The Spectrum rates these events as "affordable" and low stigma. Because these groups pull people together from moderate-sized geographic areas, it's likely that you won't know others at the event. While probably not ideal, it's possible to sit anonymously in the back row and listen. Finally, psychoeducation has been evaluated by researchers and has been found to be an effective way to promote engagement in treatment. We have thus rated the professionally led psychoeducation event as a "good" value.

Sponsors sometimes use psychoeducational events to recruit new customers for counseling, hospital, and research programs, and for new psychotropic medications. Smart consumers will be alert to self-promotional content, free take-home items bearing the sponsor's name, and other distortions of the psychoeducational content.

SELF-HELP PUBLICATIONS AND EVENTS

Although representing a wide variety of media, self-help publications and events tend to be inexpensive relative to other services and products, easy to access, "low" on the stigma, and "high" on privacy. The most reserved among us can buy or borrow a book on a mental health concern with little worry that our problems will be featured on the nine o'clock news.

The rub with self-help is that there is very little evidence that it is an effective "treatment" for any of the common mental health concerns. The exception seems to be the structured *pathway to recovery-type* workbooks, which will be discussed. On the other hand, the sales of self-help books lend some support for the idea that people get something from them. The problem is—we don't know what.

Self-help books and articles. Every library and bookstore has dozens of books on every imaginable mental health concern. Type your topic into Amazon's search box and you get scores of titles, complete with reviews by professionals and lay readers. In addition, newspapers and magazines publish hundreds of articles every year on mental health and treatment, including scholarly reviews, faddish stories on new untested treatments, testimonials, and customer-finding self-promotion. The problem with this product is clear: It's very difficult to find the trustworthy and scientifically supported factual material that we all want and need. See the sidebar on this topic for our guidelines (see Box 9.4).

Web resources.The World Wide Web is chock full of text related to mental health concerns. The most reliable content is found on government sites (e.g., nimh.gov, samhsa.gov, nih.gov), consumer advocacy group sites (e.g., DBSAlliance.org, nami.org, adaa.org), leading general medical sites (e.g., WebMD.com, healthatoz.com, Drkoop.com), and managed behavioral health organization sites (e.g., live andwork well.com, magellanassist.com, valueoptions.com/members).

CDs, DVDs, and podcasts. This category is included in the Spectrum because we expect that various organizations that have produced printed materials on mental health concerns will soon produce the content in different media such as CDs, DVDs, and podcasts. One visionary we know of, Dr. Brent Atkinson, sends pod casts, MP3 files, or CDs home with his clients to help them remember and ponder what they had worked on in their weekly sessions. You can find an example of this at his Web site at: http://www.thecouplesclinic.com/resources.htm.

Today, you can also find self-help books recorded on CDs so that you can listen to the books while doing other activities like commuting. Segments of educational television programs can already be downloaded from various network Web sites. Podcasts are downloadable files that can be transferred to portable iPods or other MP3 players and are a great way to communicate brief reminders or inspirational messages. Look to innovative counselor practices for such new products, such as Dr. Brent Atkinson.

Pathway to recovery workbooks. A number of research studies have found that printed workbooks can be effectively used to help patients manage specific mental health concerns. The Depression and Bipolar Disorder Support Alliance (dbsalliance.org) distributes one such workbook for people living with bipolar disorder. *Working Towards Wellness* is a twenty-five-page booklet that helps people identify symptoms, prioritize problems, set and track goals, prepare

BOX 9.4
Something You Should Know

Finding the best self-help materials

1. Ask friends, family members, librarians, and booksellers for recommendations.
2. Look for best-selling products on the topic of interest to you.
3. Ask a counselor, medical doctor, or a psychiatrist for a suggestion.
4. Avoid products that claim to have all the answers.
5. Avoid products that feature new and untested treatments.

for counseling and medication management visits, identify sources of peer support, and track medications. Similar workbooks can be found by searching the major consumer advocacy and government Web sites.

Recovery workbooks are most effective for people who have accepted their condition and have determined that they want to manage their care. Because not everyone enjoys paper-and-pencil participative activities, and because many don't like to admit their problems, workbooks are not for everyone. But these well-crafted and sensible tools can be helpful for the rest of us.

Journal writing. It is widely known that writing about your problems can be therapeutic. From "Dear Diary" to the blogs of cyberspace, journaling eases one's mind, gets problems "off your chest," helps a person clearly articulate the issues, and helps us plan strategies for problem solving and personal improvements. Recently, therapists have found research to support its value as a therapeutic technique in the treatment of depression and anxiety. In addition, journaling is widely used on one's own, independent of professional services.

Perhaps one of the most famous of all journal writing proponents is Dr. Ira Progoff's Intensive Journal Program for Self Development. As a practicing depth psychologist and director of the Institute for Research in Depth Psychology at Drew University from 1959 to 1971, Dr. Progoff conducted research on the dynamic process by which individuals develop more fulfilling lives. As a psychotherapist, he found that the clients who wrote in some form of a journal were able to work through issues more rapidly. Through this research, he then developed and refined the Intensive Journal method in the mid-1960s and 1970s to provide a way to mirror the processes by which people become dynamic and develop themselves.[19]

For more information regarding this well-thought-out journaling program, you can go online to: http://www.intensivejournal.org/.

For people who place high value on privacy, journaling may be particularly appealing. Those who prefer more personal interaction will find journaling wanting. For these people, journaling could be used as an adjunct to other therapy techniques. It has "low" cost, "high" ease, little stigma, and respectable value.

Recovery conferences. Alcoholics Anonymous holds regional and national meetings for AA members and their families. These conferences feature professional and lay speakers and provide a safe haven for members to share their experiences and social support. Consumer advocacy groups such as the National Alliance for the Mentally Ill, Children and Adults with Attention Deficit/Hyperactivity Disorder, and the Depression and Bipolar Disorder Support Alliance now sponsor similar events for their members and interested others. Combined, these recovery conferences can be seen as important evidence that people with mental health concerns—and their families—have begun to band together to help one another to live healthy lives *with* their mental health concerns. Although we could find no published evidence that recovery conferences reduce symptoms or promote recovery, we have little doubt that many people find such conferences meaningful and helpful. In addition, they rate well on cost, stigma, and privacy. Because there are not yet many recovery conferences, we have rated this product as "fair" for the ease dimension.

While Looking for a Purveyor of Mental Health Services

You should shop for the right clinician. Try to interview prospective clinicians over the phone. Be open with them regarding what you want and how you are feeling about the process. People come into therapy for many reasons and at different stages of readiness. If you are really interested, and want specific help, you are past the first hurdle, as readiness and willingness sets the stage for better therapy.

Spend some time, trying to understand what *you* think might help and why, before seeing a clinician. Write it out!! The trick is then to match your concerns and ideas with a person who you believe can help you. Your clinician might just have great ideas about how your circumstances might improve, so listen, and evaluate how their ideas match yours.

Questions to ask. We asked some of our clinical colleagues* what they thought someone interested in beginning therapy should ask prior to first meeting with a clinician. Here is a list of what they said; you can tailor these questions to your particular situation.

1. What professional degrees does the prospective therapist have; has he or she graduated from an accredited school of higher education? Are they licensed in the state in which you live? Do they hold multiple licenses or certificates?

---

*Our thanks to Tom Blume, Scott Christie, Karen Erickson, Stacy Overton, June Williams, Nona Leigh Wilson, and HealthsourceInfo.com on the Counselor line, for sharing their ideas with us.

2. What sort of treatment will they use, who else will be involved, and how long is treatment usually expected to last? Are recovery and after-care programs a part of the treatment plan, and how and who would provide this service? Most important, ask about costs. Even the simplest treatment, such as psychoeducational programs for first-time DUI offenders, are very expensive.

3. What are their fees and are they a participating provider for your insurance company (this tells you how much you will have to pay)?

4. How many years have they been practicing?

5. What do they consider their specialties?

6. What is their theoretical perspective?

7. Can he or she meet with you weekly (at the time that you need to meet)?

8. Do they offer a free introductory session so that you can get to know each other and determine the likelihood of a good therapeutic fit?

9. Have they done any long-term follow up with cases to find out whether or not the changes hold up once people leave counseling?

10. Can they make this stuff work in their own life? And if not, why not?

11. Have they ever counseled someone like you who ___? (Fill in the blank with things like "who is seriously depressed," "who is bisexual," "who has an eating disorder," etc.)

12. What is their perspective on diagnoses and how that information is given to the insurance company? Do they release all notes and reports? And how willing would they be to keep dialogue open about that issue? (i.e., I wouldn't want YOUR label to follow ME into the next life . . . or even through this one!).

13. If you are going to be on medication, ask:

- What are the pros and cons of this medication?
- What if the medication doesn't work?
- How long might I need to be on the medication?
- What are the side effects and what should I do about them?
- What if I decide to stop taking my medication?
- What are the benefits of medication *with* counseling and without?

14. What can you expect from her or him, and what do they expect from you in therapy?

15. What approaches will you utilize in working with my specific problems/issues?

16. How successful are these approaches for my concerns?
17. How long will it take for me to notice improvement?
18. What will you notice to tell me that I am improving?
19. Are there any potential risks to me during therapy?
20. What other types of treatments are available for my problem?
21. What are the benefits, risks, and differences in cost of these treatments?
22. Who decides when therapy is finished? What is that decision based on?
23. Do they tend to focus on what is happening in the present or on what has happened in the past that still affects the present?
24. What should you do if you don't feel that therapy is helpful?
25. What about privacy and any office and payment procedures?
26. How does their approach fit with/relate to other approaches in the field—and what evidence shows that their model is effective for this particular kind of problem? (Is there empirical support or merely testimonial?)
27. If they are proposing to use a model that is not empirically supported or is considered new or alternative, why are they doing so?
28. What exactly is the role of supervision in their work—what will get discussed and how will that benefit you?
29. How will they know when something is beyond their expertise and what will they do if it is?
30. How do they manage religious/spiritual beliefs—their own or yours—as they come up in sessions?
31. What experience do they have in understanding and helping people who are different from them in significant ways, e.g., race, gender, sexual orientation, and religious beliefs?

The American Academy of Child and Adolescent Psychiatry suggests that if you have a child or adolescent on medication, you should ask the following questions.

1. What is the name of the medication? Is it known by other names?
2. What is known about its helpfulness with other children who have a similar condition to my child?
3. How will the medication help my child? How long before I see improvement? When will it work?

4. What are the side effects that commonly occur with this medication?

5. What are the rare or serious side effects, if any, that can occur?

6. Is this medication addictive? Can it be abused?

7. What is the recommended dosage? How often will the medication be taken?

8. Are there any laboratory tests (e.g., heart tests, blood test, etc.) which need to be done before my child begins taking the medication? Will any tests need to be done while my child is taking the medication?

9. Will a child and adolescent psychiatrist be monitoring my child's response to medication and make dosage changes if necessary? How often will progress be checked and by whom?

10. Are there any foods that my child should avoid while taking the medication?

11. Are there interactions between this medication and other medications (prescription and/or over-the-counter) my child is taking?

12. Are there any activities that my child should avoid while taking the medication? Are any precautions recommended for other activities?

13. How long will my child need to take this medication? How will the decision be made to stop this medication?

14. What do I do if a problem develops (e.g., if my child becomes ill, doses are missed, or side effects develop)?

15. What is the cost of the medication (generic versus brand name)?

16. Does my child's school nurse need to be informed about this medication?[20]

The Bottom Line

And so, you can see that there are many people to help you, and things you can do to take the place of therapy, forestall your involvement, and add to or supplement your mental health care. You have learned about the mysteries of mental health services that the field seems to keep locked away from you, the many types of treatments, the differences and similarities of all the practitioners, and alternatives that can help, even though they may not now be a commonly recognized part of the field.

When you think of it, there are many people who probably could use some therapy, but seem to get by without it. How do they do it? They take advantage of the help that is already available to them.

Some live in disquieting anxiety and desperation, but many of them make do and go on to better lives. It is our hope that this book has given you enough information to make informed choices. Our wish is that you will have better living and improved mental health.

Post Script

After writing and then reviewing this book, several issues strike us. First, we think we should advocate harder for a wider range of services to be legitimized by the whole field of mental health, like those we put forth in the Spectrum. Next, we believe there should be more research dollars given to prevention and investigation of alternatives. We were sort of tickled that, over the course of writing this book, a few types of treatments that we once believed to have limited positive research outcomes finally came of age. This demonstrates for us, the continual changes that happen in the field, adding to our challenge in getting the word out to those in need. We believe that costs for treatments should be made affordable *for all* rather than just those who have insurance for mental health care, *and* that the field should work toward a cleaner, clearer view of what is helpful for which sorts of problems at the lowest cost, rather than a one-size-fits-all system. The use of the term "health care" may be wrongly used; many of the problems being treated are psycho-social-familial. The vernacular of mental health "code words" requires clinicians to lie/skew the diagnosis in order to fit it into the current system, and that does not help those who are treated, those who treat, and those who provide benefits.

We believe that these changes will not come about naturally from within the system, but will need a grassroots nudge from every consumer, every person who needs services but cannot afford them, and from every clinician who cares.

Notes

Introduction

1. Smith, M.L., Glass, G.W., & Miller, T.I. (1986). *The Benefits of Psychotherapy.* Baltimore: Johns Hopkins University Press.

2. Stiles, W.B., Shapiro, D.A., & Elliot, R. (1986). Are all psychotherapies equivalent? *American Psychologist,* 41, 165-180.

Chapter One

1. Horney, K. (1937). *The Neurotic Personality of our Time.* New York: W.W. Norton, pp. 14-15.

2. Wylie, M.S. (2004). Mindsight: Dan Siegel offers therapists a new vision of the brain. *Psychotherapy Networker,* September/October.

3. American Psychiatric Association. (2000). *Diagnostic and Statistical Manual of Mental Disorders.* (Fourth Edition), Text Revision. Washington, DC: American Psychiatric Association.

4. Gergen, K. J. (1991). *The Saturated Self.* New York: Basic Books.

5. Sahler, O.J Z., & Carr, J.E., (Eds.), (2003). *The Behavioral Sciences and Health Care.* Cambridge, MA: Hogrefe & Huber.

6. Swenson, L.C. (1997). *Psychology and Law for the Helping Professions.* (Second Ed.). Pacific Grove, CA: Brooks/Cole.

7. Durlak, J.A. (1998). Common risk and protective factors in successful prevention programs. *American Journal of Orthopsychiatry,* 68, 512-520.

8. Scovern, A.W. (1999). From Placebo to Alliance: The Role of Common Factors in Medicine. In M. Hubble, B. Duncan and S. Miller (Eds.). *The Heart and Soul of Change: What Works in Therapy.* Washington, DC: American Psychological Association.

9. Ibid.

10. Sackett, D.L. & Snow, J.C. (1979). *Compliance in Health Care.* Baltimore: Johns Hopkins University Press.

11. Cosgrove, L., Krimsky, S., & Vijayaraghavan, M. (2006). Financial ties between DSM-IV panel members and the pharmaceutical industry. *Psychotherapy and Psychosomatics,* 75, 154-156.

Chapter Two

1. Seligman M.E.P. & Csikszentmihalyi, M. (2000). Positive Psychology. *American Psychologist,* 55, 1, 5-14.

2. Edwards, J.K. & Pyskoty, C.E. (2004). Clinical training needs of Illinois counselors: A survey of internship sites. *Illinois Counseling Association Journal.*

3. Ogles, B.M., Anderson, T., & Lunnen, K.M. (2001). The contribution of models and techniques to therapeutic efficacy: Contradictions between professional trends and clinical research. In M. Hubble, B. Duncan and S. Miller (Eds). *The Heart and Soul of Change: What Works in Therapy.* Washington, DC: American Psychological Association.

4. Lewis, J. A., Lewis, M.D., Daniels, J.A., & D'Andrea, M.J. (2003). *Community Counseling Empowerment Strategies for a Diverse Society.* Pacific Grove, CA: Brooks/Cole.

5. Albee, G.W., & Ryan-Finn, K.D. (1993). An overview of primary prevention. *Journal of Counseling and Development,* 72, 115-121.

6. Asay, T.P., & Lambert, M. J. (1999). The Empirical Case for the Common Factors in Therapy: Quantitative Findings. In M. Hubble, B. Duncan and S. Miller, (Eds.) *The Heart and Soul of Change: What Works in Therapy.* Washington, DC: American Psychological Association.

7. Seligman, M.E.P. (2002). *Authentic Happiness.* New York: The Free Press.

8. Seligman, M.E.P. (1993). *What You Can Change and What You Can't.* New York: Fawcett Books.

Chapter Three

1. Bowen, M. (1978). *Family Therapy in Clinical Practice.* New York: Jason Aronson.

2. Pinsof, W.M., & Wynne, L.C. (1995). The effectiveness and efficacy of marital and family therapy: Introduction to the special issue. *Journal of Marital and Family Therapy,* 21, 341-344.

3. Wetchler, J. L., & Piercy, F. P. (1996). Transgenerational Family Therapies. In F. Piercy, D. Sprenkle and J. Wetchler (Eds.). *Family Therapy Sourcebook.* (Second Ed.). New York: The Guilford Press.

4. Bowen, M. (1974). Toward the differentiation of self in one's family of origin. In *Georgetown Family Symposium,* Vol. 1, Andres and J. Lorio, (Eds.) Washington, DC: Department of Psychiatry, Georgetown University Medical Center.

5. Stanton, M.D. & Todd, T.C. (1982). *The Family Therapy of Drug Abuse and Addiction.* New York: The Guilford Press.

6. Meyers, R.J., Apodaca, T.R., Flicker, S.M., & Slesnick, N. (2002). Evidence-based approaches for the treatment of substance abusers by involving family members. *Family Journal: Counseling & Therapy for Couples & Families,* 10(3), 281-288.

7. Nichols, M.P. & Schwartz, R.C. (2001). *Family Therapy: Concepts and Methods.* (Fifth Edition). Boston: Allyn Bacon.

8. White, M. (1984). Pseudo-encopresis: From avalanche to victory; from vicious to virtuous cycles. *Family Systems Medicine,* 2 (2): 150-160.

9. Freedman, J. & Combs, G. (1996). *Narrative Therapy: The Social Construction of Preferred Realities.* New York: W.W. Norton, Company, Inc.

10. Hubble, M.A., Duncan, B.L., & Miller, S.D. (1999). Introduction. In M. Hubble, B. Duncan and S. Miller (Eds.) *The Heart and Soul of Change: What Works in Therapy.* Washington, DC: American Psychological Association.

11. Barlett, D.L. & Steele, J.B. (2004). *Critical Condition: How Health Care in America Became Big Business and Bad Medicine.* New York: Doubleday.

Chapter Four

1. Durlak, J.A. (1979). Comparative effectiveness of paraprofessionals and professional helpers. *Psychological Bulletin,* 86(1), 80-92.

2. Berman, J.A., & Norton, N.C. (1985). Does professional training make a therapist more effective? *Psychological Bulletin,* 98(2), 401-407.

3. Rowe, C.L. & Liddle, H.A. (2003). Substance abuse. *Journal of Marital & Family Therapy,* 29, 97-120.

4. Moderation Management. Retrieved July 10, 2006 from, http://www.moderation.org/.

5. Hersey, B. (2001). *The Controlled Drinking Debates: A Review of Four Decades of Acrimony.* Retrieved July 10, 2006 from, http://www.doctordeluca.com/Library/AbstinenceHR/FourDecadesAcrimony.htm.

6. NAADAC. Retrieved July, 23, 2005 from, http://www.naadac.org/.

7. American Counseling Association. Retrieved July, 23, 2005 from, http://www.counseling.org Home/Faq.aspx/.

8. National Association of Social Workers. Retrieved July, 23, 2005 from, http://www.naswdc.org/.

9. American Psychotherapy and Medical Hypnosis Association. APMHA Web site. Retrieved April 10, 2007 from, http://apmha.com/aboutAPMHA.htm.

10. American Association for Marriage and Family Therapy. Retrieved July, 23, 2005 from, http://www.aamft.org/faqs/index_nm.asp#who.

11. American Association for Pastoral Counselors. Retrieved January 8, 2004 from, http://www.aapc.org/practice.htm.

12. Ibid.

13. International Coaching Federation. *What is Coaching?* Retrieved May 1, 2006 from, http://www.coachfederation.org/ICF/For+Coaching+Clients/What+is+a+Coach/.

14. The Commission on Rehabilitation Certification. Retrieved January 8, 2004 from, http://www.crccertification.com/downloads/35scope/scope_of_practice.pdf.

15. Breggin, P. (1991). *Toxic Psychiatry.* New York: St. Martin's Press.

16. Psychiatry. Encyclopædia Britannica Online. Retrieved December 12, 2003 from, http://www.search.eb.com/eb/article?eu=63280.

17. Steinberg, H. A short history of psychiatry at Leipzg University. Retrieved January 2, 2004 from, http://www.uni-leipzig.de/~psy/eng/geschi-e.htm.

18. American Psychiatric Association. Retrieved January 4, 2004 from, www.psych.org.

19. American Psychiatric Association. Retrieved January 4, 2004 from, http://www.psych.org/public_info/what_psych.cfm.

20. Breggin, P. (1991). *Toxic Psychiatry.* New York: St. Martin's Press.

21. Andreasen, N. (1984). *The Broken Brain: The Biological Revolution in Psychiatry.* New York: Harper and Row, Publishers, Inc.

22. Ibid.

23. Stevenson, D. (1996). *Sigmund Freud: The Father of Psychoanalysis.* Brown University. Retrieved January 10, 2004 from, http://65.107.211.206/science/freud/Biography.html.

24. Whitefield, W. (2003). Understanding the biological bases of mental illness. *International Journal of Psychiatric Nursing Research,* 9, 1.

25. Nursing. Encyclopædia Britannica. Retrieved December 16, 2003 from, Encyclopædia Britannica Online. Retrieved January 23, 2004 from, http://www.search.eb.com/eb/article?eu=119081.

26. American Psychological Association (APA). Defintion of Psychologist; Definition of Psychology. Retrieved February 1, 2004 from, www.apa.org./about/?imw=Y.

27. Seligman, M.E.P. & Csikszentmihalyi, M. (2000). Positive psychology. *American Psychologist,* 55, 5-14.

28. Seligman, M.E.P. (1998). Building human strength: Psychology's forgotten mission. *APA Monitor,* 29, 1 (January). Retrieved February 2, 2004 from, http://www.apa.org/monitor/jan98/pres.html. Copyright 1998 by the American Psychological Association. Reprinted with permission.

29. Ibid.

30. Seligman, M.E.P. (1998). Building human strength: Psychology's forgotten mission. *APA Monitor,* 29, 1 (January). Retrieved February 2, 2004 from, http://www.apa.org/monitor/jan98/pres.html.

31. *Mental Health: A Report of the Surgeon General.* Chapter 1, Introduction and Themes: Mental Health and Mental Illness: Points on a Continuum. Retrieved February 2, 2004 from, http://www.surgeongeneral.gov/library/mentalhealth/ chapter1/sec1.html.

Chapter Five

1. Smith, M.L., Glass, G.W., & Miller, T.I. (1986). *The Benefits of Psychotherapy.* Baltimore: Johns Hopkins University Press.

2. Chen, M.W. & Rybak, C. J. (2003). *Group Leadership Skills: Interpersonal Process in Group Counseling and Therapy.* Belmont, CA: Brooks/Cole.

3. Edwards, J.K. (2002). An Investigation into the State of the Art and Current Needs for the Clinical Training of Behavioral Health Care Professionals in the United States Across Disciplines and Within Clinical Training Sites. *Northeastern Illinois, 2001-02 University Committee on Research Grant,* Unpublished manuscript.

4. Edwards, J.K. & Pyskote, C. (2004). Clinical training needs of counselors in Illinois: A survey of clinical internship sites. *The Journal of the Illinois Counseling Association.*

5. Raskin, N.J. & Rogers, C.R. (2004), (Seventh edition). Person-centered therapy. In R. Corsini, and D. Wedding (Eds.). *Current psychotherapies.* Stamford, CT: Wadsworth, Inc.

6. Smith, M.L., Glass, G.W., & Miller, T.I. (1986). *The Benefits of Psychotherapy.* Baltimore: Johns Hopkins University Press.

7. Ibid.

8. Weiner-Davis, M., deShazer, S., & Gingerich, W. (1987). Building on pretreatment change to construct the therapeutic solution: An exploratory study. *Journal of Marital and Family Therapy,* 14(4), 359-364.

9. Prochaska, J.O. (1999). How do people change, and how can we change to help many more people? In M. Hubble, B. Duncan and S. Miller (Eds.). *The Heart and Soul of Change: What Works in Therapy.* Washington, DC: American Psychological Association.

10. Schwarzbaum, S. E. (2004). Low-income Latinos and dropout: Strategies to prevent dropout. *Journal of Multicultural Counseling and Development,* 32, 296-306.

11. Lambert, M.J. & Bergin, A.E. (1994). The effectiveness of psychotherapy: In A.E. Bergin & S.L. Garfield (Eds.), *Handbook of psychotherapy and behavior change.* (Fourth edition). New York: Wiley.

12. Lambert, M. J. & Anderson, E. M. (1996). Assessment for the time-limited psychotherapies. *Review of Psychiatry,* pp. 23-42. Washington, DC: American Psychiatric Press, Inc.

13. Andrews, G., Tennant, C., Hewson, D., & Schonell, M. (1978). The relation of social factors to physical and psychiatric Illness. *American Journal of Epidemiology,* 27-35.

14. Gaston, L. (1990). The concept of the alliance and its role in psychotherapy: Theoretical and empirical considerations. *Psychotherapy,* 27, 143-153.

15. Rosenthal, R. & Jacobson, L. (1968). *Pygmalion in the Classroom.* New York: Holt, Rinehart & Winston.

16. Howard, K.L., Kopta, S.M., Krause, M.S., & Orlinsky, D.E. (1986). The dose-effect relationship in psychotherapy. *American Psychologist,* 41, 159-164.

17. Edwards, J.K. & Pyskote, C. (2004). Clinical training needs of counselors in Illinois: A survey of clinical internship sites. *The Journal of the Illinois Counseling Association.*

18. Olfson, M., Marcus, S.C., & Druss, B. (2002). National trends in the outpatient treatment of depression. *Journal of the American Medical Association,* 287, 203-209.

19. Saulny, S. (Sept 1, 2005). Goodbye Therapist. Hello Anxiety. *New York Times.* Retrieved September 24, 2005 from, http://nytimes.com/2005/09/01/fashion/thursdaystyles/01THERAPY.HTML?ei+5070&.

Chapter Six

1. Sahler, O.J.Z., & Carr, J.E. (2003) (Eds.). Evolving Models of Health Care. *The Behavioral Sciences and Health Care.* Cambridge, MA: Hogrefe & Huber.

2. Coyne, J.C., Linickman, M.S., & Nease, D.E. (2002). Emotional disorders in primary care. *Journal of Consulting and Clinical Psychology,* 70, 798-809.

3. National Depressive and Manic Depressive Association. *Beyond diagnosis: A landmark survey of depression and treatment.* Retrieved 2001, January 22, 2004 from, http://www.dbsalliance.org/bookstore/brochures.html.

4. Seligman, M.E.P. (2002). *Authentic Happiness.* New York: Free Press.

5. Seligman, M.E.P. (1993). *What You Can Change, and What You Can't.* New York: Ballantine Publishing Group.

6. Olfson, M., Marcus, S.C., & Druss, B. (2002). National trends in the outpatient treatment of depression. *Journal of the American Medical Association,* 287, 203-209.

7. Gray, G.V., Brody, D.S., & Johnson, D. (2005). The evolution of behavioral primary care. *Professional Psychology: Research and Practice.* American Psychological Association, 36, 123-129 (p. 124).

8. Albee, G.W. & Ryan-Finn, K.D. (1993). An overview of primary prevention. *Journal of Counseling and Development,* 72, 115-121.

9. Sahler, O.J.Z., & Carr, J.E. (2003) (Eds.). *The Behavioral Sciences and Health Care.* Cambridge, MA: Hogrefe & Huber.

10. American Psychiatric Association. (2000). *Diagnostic and Statistical Manual of Mental Disorders,* Fourth Edition, Text Revision. Washington, DC: Author. p. xxx.

11. Ibid., p. xxxi.

12. Duncan, B.L., Miller, S.D., & Sparks, J.A., et al. (2004). The Myth of the Magic Pill: The ethics and Science of medication. In B. Duncan, S. Miller, and J. Sparks (Eds.). *The Heroic Client.* San Francisco: Jossey Bass.

13. Ibid.

14. GlaxoSmithKline. (1997-2006). *PaxilCR.* Retrieved Tuesday, October 18, 2005 from, http://www.paxilcr.com.

15. *National Institute of Mental Health—Publication Materials*—Medications. Retrieved December 14, 2005 from, http://www.nimh.nih.gov/publicat/pubListing.cfm?dID=35.

16. Healthyplace.com. *Psychiatric Medications Overview*-Retrieved December 14, 2005 from, http://www.healthyplace.com/site/psychiatric_medications.htm 12/14/2005.

17. Narrow W.E., Rae D.S., & Regier D.A. (1998). *NIMH epidemiology note*: Prevalence of anxiety disorders. One-year prevalence best estimates calculated from ECA and NCS data. Population estimates based on U.S. Census estimated residential population age 18 to 54 on July 1, 1998. Unpublished.

18. National Institute of Mental Health. *Teenage Brain: A Work in Progress.* Retrieved February 6, 2006 from, http://www.nimh.nih.gov/publicat/teenbrain.cfm.

19. Breggin, P. (1991). Suppressing the passion of children with hospitalization and with drugs, such as Ritaline and Mellaril. In P. Breggin (Ed.), *Toxic Psychiatry.* New York: St. Martin's Press.

20. National Institute of Mental Health—Publications. *Attention Deficit Hyperactivity Disorder.* Retrieved March 12, 2006 from, http://www.nimh.nih.gov/publicat/pubListing.cfm?dID=14.

21. National Institute of Mental Health—*Antidepressant Medications for Children and Adolescents: Information for Parents and Caregivers.* Retrieved March 12, 2006 from, http://www.nimh.nih.gov/healthinformation/antidepressant_child.cfm.

22. U.S. Food and Drug Administration, Center for Drug Evaluation and Research. *Antidepressant Use in Children, Adolescents and Adults*. Retrieved December 15, 2005 from, http://www.fda.gov/cder/drug/antidepressants/.

Chapter Seven

1. Corey, G., Corey, M.S., & Callanan, P. (2003). *Issues and Ethics in the Helping Professions.* Pacific Grove, CA: Brooks/Cole.

2. Wheeler and Bertram's ACA Workshop (as cited in Corry, Corry, and Callanan's *Issues and Ethics in the Helping Professions.* Pacific Grove, CA: Brooks/Cole (p. 154).

3. Knapp, S. (1997). Ethical and Legal Aspects of Clinical Supervision. In C. Edward Watkins (Ed.), *Handbook of Psychotherapy Supervision,* New York: John Wiley & Sons, Inc.

4. Bachmann, KM., Bossi, J., Moggi, F., Stirnemann-Lewis, F., Sommer, R., & Brenner, H.D. (2000). Nurse-patient sexual contact in psychiatric hospitals. *Archives of Sexual Behavior,* 29(4).

5. Hubble, M.A., Duncan, B.L., and Miller, S.D. (1999). Introduction. In M. Hubble, B. Duncan and S. Miller *The Heart and Soul of Change: What Works in Therapy.* Washington, DC: American Psychological Association.

6. False Memory Syndrome Foundation. Retrieved March 27, 2006 from, http://www.fmsfonline.org/fmsffaq.html.

7. Hubble, M.A., Duncan, B.L., & miller, S.D. (1999). Introduction. In M. Hubble, B. Duncan, & S. Miller, *The Heart and Soul of Change: What Works in Therapy.* Washington, DC: American Psychological Association.

8. Levinson, W., Roter, D.L., Mullooly, J.P., Dull, V.T., and Frankel, R.M. (1997). Physician-patient communication: The relationship with malpractice claims among primary care physicians and surgeons. *Journal of the American Medical Association,* 277, 7, 553-559.

9. Charles, S.C., Gibbons, R.D., Frisch, P.R., Pyskoty, C.E., Hedeker, D., and Singha, N.K. (1992). Predicting risk for medical malpractice claims using quality-of-care characteristics. *West Journal of Medicine.* 157(4), 433-439.

10. American Board of Professional Psychology. Retrieved April 2, 2006 from, http://www.abpp.org/brochures/general_brochure.htm 03/17/2006.

11. Edwards, J.K. (2005). Advanced Skills (Thinking) in Clinical Supervision: From Effectiveness to Greatness in Supervision. Paper presented at The First International Interdisciplinary Conference on Clinical Supervision. University of New York at Buffalo, Amherst, New York.

Chapter Eight

1. Himmelstein, DU, Warren, E., Thorne, D., Woolhandler, S. (2005). Market-Watch: Illness and injury as contributors to bankruptcy. *Health Affairs,* 2005 Jan-June; Suppl Web Exclusives W5-63-W5-73.

2. Saleem, H. T. New law moves insurance plans closer to total mental health parity. *Bureau of Labor Statistics.* Retrieved November 20, 2006 from, http://www.bls.gov/opub/cwc/print/cm20030909ar01pl.htm.

3. National Mental Health Association. *What Have States Done to Ensure Health Insurance Parity?* Retrieved April 25, 2006 from, http://www.nmha.org/state/parity/state_parity.cfm.

4. Bureau of Labor Statistics. *Trends in Health Insurance.* Retrieved August 1, 2006 from, http://www.bls.gov/opub/ted/2000/May/wk3/art02.htm.

5. Gray, G. V., Brody, D.S., & Johnson, D, (2005). The evolution of behavioral primary care. *Professional Psychology: Research and Practice.* 36 (2), 123-129.

6. Ignagni, K. (2006). $6,280 and counting. Coverage. *American Health Insurance Plans,* p. 7.

Chapter Nine

1. White, M. & Epston, D. (1990). *Narrative Means to Therapeutic Ends.* New York: Guilford Press.

2. M. Scott Peck, (1989). *The Road Less Traveled.* New York: Simon and Schuster.

3. American Nurses Association. *The Registered Nurse Population. Findings from the National Sample Survey of Registered Nurses,* March 2004, U.S. Department of Health & Human Services, Public Health Service, Division of Nursing, Health Resources Services Administration. Retrieved 05/13/06 from, http://www.nursingworld.org/readroom/fsadvprc.htm.

4. U.S. Department of Health and Human Services. *Preliminary Findings: 2004 National Sample Survey of Registered Nurses.* Retrieved 05/13/06 from, http://bhpr.hrsa.gov/healthworkforce/reports/rnpopulation/preliminaryfindings.htm.

5. International Coach Federation. *What is Coaching?* Retrieved May 1, 2006 from, http://www.coachfederation.org/ICF/For+Coaching+Clients/What+is+a+Coach/.

6. Family Village Library. How to Start a Self-Help / Support Group. Retrieved May 4, 2006 from, http://www.familyvillage.wisc.edu/general/selfhelp.html.

7. Moyers, T.B. & Hester, R.K. (1999). Outcome research: Alcoholism. In M. Galanter & H. Kleber (Eds.), *Textbook of Substance Abuse Treatment* (pp. 129-134). Washington, DC: American Psychiatric Press.

8. Miller, W.R., Meyers, R.J. & Tonigan, J.S. (1999). Engaging the unmotivated in treatment for alcohol problems: A comparison of three strategies for intervention through family members. *Journal of Consulting and Clinical Psychology,* 688-97.

9. Disease Management Association of America. *Definition of DM.* Retrieved May 15, 2006 from, http://www.dmaa.org/definition.html.

10. Schwarzbaum, S. (2004). Low-income Latinos and drop out: Strategies to prevent dropout. *Journal of Multicultural Counseling and Development,* 32, 296-306.

11. Asay, R.P. & Lambert, M. J. (1999). The empirical case for the common factors in therapy: Quantitative Findings. In M. Hubble, B. Duncan and S. Miller (Eds.), *The Heart and Soul of Change: What Works in Therapy.* Washington DC: American Psychological Association.

12. Andrews, G., Tennant, C., Hewson, D., & Schonell, M. (1978). The relation of social factors to physical and psychiatric illness. *American Journal of Epidemiology,* 27-35.

13. Stephen Ministry, St. Louis. *History of Stephen Ministry.* Retrieved May 2, 2006 from, http://www.stephenministries.org/.

14. Weil, A. (1995). *Spontaneous Healing*. New York: Fawcett Columbine.

15. SAMHSA National Mental Health Information Center, Retrieved May, 1, 2006 from, http://www.mentalhealth.samhsa.gov/publications/allpubs/ken98-0044/default.asp#what.

16. Weiner, M. A., & Weiner, J. (1994). *Herbs that Heal.* CA: Quantum Books.

17. Tierra, M. (1980). *The Way of Herbs*. New York: Pocket Books.

18. Gardner-Gordon, J. (1995). Managing Fear, Pain, and Depression with Kava. *The Herbalist:* Newsletter of the American Herbalists Guild, November, 19.

19. The Progroff Intensive Journal Program, About Dr. Progroff. Retrieved May 22, 2006 from, http://www.intensivejournal.org/about/aboutProgoff.php.

20. American Academy of Child and Adolescent Psychiatry, *Psychiatric Medication for Children and Adolescents Part III: Questions to Ask* (2004) Retrieved April 5, 2006 from, http://www.aacap.org/publications/factsfam/medquest.htm.

References

American Academy of Child and Adolescent Psychiatry. *Psychiatric Medication For Children And Adolescents Part I-How Medications Are Used: Facts for Families* No. 21. Retrieved July 12, 2006 from, www.aacap.org.

American Psychiatric Association. (2000). *Diagnostic and Statistical Manual of Mental Disorders.* Fourth Edition, Text Revision. Washington, DC: APA.

Barlett, D.B. & Steele, J.B. (2006). *Critical Condition.* New York: Broadway Books.

Corey, G., Corey, M.S., & Callanan, P. (2003). *Issues and Ethics in the Helping Professions.* Pacific Grove, CA: Brooks/Cole.

Duncan, B.J., Miller, S.D., & Sparks, J.A. (2004). *The Heroic Client: A Revolutionary Way to Improve Effectiveness through Client-Directed, Outcome-Informed Therapy.* San Francisco: Jossey-Bass.

Gergen, K. J. (1991). *The Saturated Self.* New York: Basic Books.

Hawking, S. (1996). *A Brief History of Time.* New York: Bantam Books.

Hubble, M.A., Duncan, B.L, & Miller, S.D. (2001). Questions from the Editors. In M. Hubble, B. Duncan, & S. Miller, (Eds.), *The Heart and Soul of Change: What Works Therapy.* Washington, DC: American Psychological Association.

Kataoka, S.H., Zhang, L., & Wells, K.B. (2002). Unmet needs for mental health care among U.S. Children: Variations by ethnicity and insurance status. *Psychiatry,* 159: 1548-1555.

Maslow, A.H. (2000). (Edited by Deborah Stephens) *The Maslow Business Reader.* Hoboken, NJ: John Wiley and Sons.

May, G. (1990). *Simply Sane: The Spirituality of Mental Health.* New York: Crossroads Publishing Co.

Mental Health: A Report of the Surgeon General. Introduction. Retrieved March 22, 2007 from, http://download.ncadi.samhsa.gov/ken/pdf/surgeon generalreport/C1.pdf.

Nichol, M.P. with Schwartz, R.C. (2006). *Family Therapy: Concepts and Methods.* Boston, MA: Allyn & Bacon.

Nichol, M.P. with Schwartz, R.C. (2007). *The Essentials of Family Therapy,* Boston, MA: Allyn & Bacon.

Quotation Details: *Lord Byron.* Retrieved March 11, 2007 from The Quotations Page: http://www.quotationspage.com/quote/2598.html.

Quotations Book.com. Williams, Bern. Retrieved March 12, 2007 from the Authors Page: http://www.quotationsbook.com/author/7731/.

Reiger, D.A., Narrow, W.E., Rae, D.S., Manderscheid, R.W., Lock, B.Z., & Goodwin, F.K. (1993). The de facto US mental and addictive disorders service system. Epidemiologic Catchment Area prospective 1-year prevalence rates of disorders and service. *Archives of General Psychiatry*, 50, 85-94.

Seligman, M.E.P. (2001). Comment of "priorities for prevention research at NIMH." *Prevention and Treatment*, 4, 24, posted June 26, 2001. Retrieved September 8, 2003 from the American Psychological Association http://journals.apa.org/prevention/volu,e4/pre0040024c.html.

Seligman, M. E.P. (2002). *Authentic Happiness*. New York: Free Press.

Walsh, F. (Ed.), (2003). *Normal Family Process: Growing Diversity and Complexity*. New York: Guilford Press.

Walter, J.L. & Peller, J.E. (1992). *Becoming Solution-Focused in Brief Therapy*. New York:Brunner/Mazel.

Wylie, M.S. (2004). Mindsight: Dan Siegel offers therapists a new vision of the brain. *Psychotherapy Networker*, September/October, pp. 29-39.

Index

("b" indicates boxed material; "i" indicates an illustration; "t" indicates a table)